The Kitchen Devotional

Readings and Recipes to Feed Your Soul,
Nourish Your Faith, and Bring Joy to the Table

BAKER PUBLISHING GROUP

Revell

a division of Baker Publishing Group
Grand Rapids, Michigan

© 2024 by Baker Publishing Group

Published by Revell
a division of Baker Publishing Group
Grand Rapids, Michigan
RevellBooks.com

Printed in China

Library of Congress Cataloging-in-Publication Data

Names: Baker Publishing Group, editor.

Title: The kitchen devotional : readings and recipes to feed your soul, nourish your faith, and bring joy to the table / Baker Publishing Group.

Description: Grand Rapids, Michigan : Revell, a division of Baker Publishing Group, [2024] | Includes bibliographical references.

Identifiers: LCCN 2023058741 | ISBN 9780800746315 (cloth) | ISBN 9781493447091 (ebook)

Subjects: LCSH: Food—Religious aspects—Christianity. | Cooking—Religious aspects—Christianity. | Dinners and dining—Religious aspects—Christianity. | Interpersonal relations—Religious aspects—Christianity. | LCGFT: Cookbooks.

Classification: LCC BR115.N87 K57 2024 | DDC 242/.2—dc23/eng/20240126

LC record available at https://lccn.loc.gov/2023058741

Unless otherwise indicated, Scripture quotations are from the Holy Bible, New International Version®, NIV®. Copyright © 1973, 1978, 1984, 2011 by Biblica, Inc.® Used by permission of Zondervan. All rights reserved worldwide. www.zondervan.com. The "NIV" and "New International Version" are trademarks registered in the United States Patent and Trademark Office by Biblica, Inc.®

Scripture quotations labeled AMP are from the Amplified Bible. Copyright © 2015 by The Lockman Foundation. Used by permission. www.lockman.org

Scripture quotations labeled CEV are from the Contemporary English Version. Copyright © 1991, 1992, 1995 by American Bible Society. Used by permission.

Scripture quotations labeled ESV are from The Holy Bible, English Standard Version® (ESV®). Copyright © 2001 by Crossway, a publishing ministry of Good News Publishers. Used by permission. All rights reserved. ESV Text Edition: 2016

Scripture quotations labeled KJV are from the King James Version of the Bible.

Scripture quotations labeled Message are from *The Message*. Copyright © 1993, 2002, 2018 by Eugene H. Peterson. Used by permission of NavPress. All rights reserved. Represented by Tyndale House Publishers.

Scripture quotations labeled NASB are from the (NASB®) New American Standard Bible®. Copyright © 1960, 1971, 1977, 1995, 2020 by The Lockman Foundation. Used by permission. All rights reserved. www.lockman.org

Scripture quotations labeled NKJV are from the New King James Version®. Copyright © 1982 by Thomas Nelson. Used by permission. All rights reserved.

Scripture quotations labeled NLT are from the *Holy Bible*, New Living Translation. Copyright © 1996, 2004, 2015 by Tyndale House Foundation. Used by permission of Tyndale House Publishers, Carol Stream, Illinois 60188. All rights reserved.

Scripture quotations labeled TLB are from *The Living Bible*. Copyright © 1971 by Tyndale House Foundation. Used by permission of Tyndale House Foundation, Carol Stream, Illinois 60188. All rights reserved.

Interior design by Jane Klein.
Cover design by Laura Klynstra.

Note: all recipe temperatures are in degrees Fahrenheit.

24   25   26   27   28   29   30   7   6   5   4   3   2   1

Contents

SECTION 5   THE MINISTRY OF HOSPITALITY

SECTION 6 THE RECIPE FOR SOUL CARE

Introduction

My parents have enjoyed vegetable gardening for most of their married life. My sister and I would be roped into helping to pick, snap, peel, shuck, and cook all of the produce their small garden yielded each summer. It wasn't my favorite chore when I was a kid, but I enjoy helping them with it now as an adult. Even though I live a couple hundred miles away from my parents, I am still a beneficiary of their hard work as Mom will send me home with canned beans and peas and bags of fresh ears of corn. It serves as good motivation to lend them a hand with the garden when I visit.

This past summer, as my mom and I were sitting on their back porch snapping green beans, my dad commented that he had a picture of my mom and my grandmother sitting in the exact spot, doing the same task the year before Grandmom passed away. He took a photo of my mom and me to capture the new scene while we all remembered the past.

My grandmother was a woman of deep faith and selfless service to her family, church, and neighbors. Her love for us was often conveyed through a table full of made-from-scratch dishes, from her legendary yeast rolls with strawberry preserves to decadent desserts of pies, cakes, and candies. She knew what each of us liked and always strove to make us something special when we were together.

A simple bushel of green beans brought back my connection with Grandmom and the love I have for her.

Few things in life generate connections like food. Whether it's preparing a meal, gathering people around a table, taking a dish to a sick friend, or swapping recipes within the family, food is the common denominator in many relationships. It's the icebreaker to meetups, first dates, and church potlucks.

It's the delicious thread that keeps memories of loved ones and special events alive. Food is also one of the best evangelism tools at our disposal. Gospel conversations don't seem so intimidating when we're sharing a meal with someone. Yes, food is a powerful connector.

This collection of devotions will remind you how food can do more than fill an empty stomach. It can bring joy and fun to your kitchen while nourishing and satisfying your soul. The readings are grouped into some of the ways food ministers to us and others, both around a table and beyond. We hope you'll be inspired to see food as the catalyst to happy gatherings, sweet memories, personal refreshment, and new insights into God's timeless Word.

The recipes are an assortment of favorite dishes that have fed our friends and families over the years, and we hope they'll be enjoyed by your favorite people too. So pull up a chair to our table or hop on a stool at our kitchen counter. Join us as we share stories, encouragement, and a good helping of faith to inspire you in and out of the kitchen.

Rachel McRae, editor

A Gathering of Family and Friends

Tastes Like Home

ANDREA DOERING

. . . .

For every house is built by someone, but God is the builder of everything.
Hebrews 3:4

When our children were growing up, they were allowed (within reason) to pick what they wanted to have for their birthday dinner. The girls always chose to go out to dinner. And most years Henry could be swayed by his twin sister, who had more definite ideas.

But Henry's preference was a meal at home. He had simple but definite tastes, and when it was his choice, he wanted homemade mashed potatoes and gravy, macaroni and cheese, and the rarest of all—a Shirley Temple to drink, loaded with maraschino cherries. And though he didn't say so, I think he also liked the relaxed dress code and zero travel time that went along with dinner at home. No one would tell him to hurry up and get in the car, and no one would require a collared shirt for a meal at home. (He and I still chuckle about his resistance to collared shirts, which would often turn into a deeply philosophical discussion aimed at wearing me down.)

Meals at home were also my dad's favorite. When it was his choice on where to have his birthday dinner, it was steak and salad at home, with pineapple upside-down cake for dessert. And while my menu of choice might differ, I understand this love of meals at home. For me, home is the location of a great meal.

Like Henry and my dad, my days as a kid were spent at public school—which meant cafeteria meals. Those meals fill you up, and they are shared companionably for the most part with people in the same boat. After school, we were all watched by someone else, in someone else's home, while our moms worked. We had a good time, and the meals were good. But it was not home.

The meals with family, around our own table, in our own spots—that seemed to make all three of us the happiest. Regardless of what was on the menu, it was going to be a great meal. It wasn't a place where we had to be; it wasn't a place where we were guests. It was the place where we belonged. The more I learned of my dad's childhood, the more I realized how important this was. For a time, he and his sister lost their home—they were sent to live in an orphanage during a rough patch in their family, while their father scrambled to bring their finances back in order. During those years, they had each other but no home—no place at a table to call their own. When I learned that, I came to understand in a new way why he insisted we each have our own place, and why he loved a home-cooked meal most of all.

God uses the fact of families, and the rhythm of families, in mysterious ways to create humans with a strong sense of their identity as children of God. It also seems so simple—a meal, a seat we can call our own, a group of people whom we identify as ours—our mom, our dad, our child. It's such an elegant scaffolding on which to build a life that we often miss it. We can tell ourselves these moments don't matter. But they do. They allow us, from that place of belonging, to extend ourselves to others and help them belong as well.

Room at the Table for Everyone

EMMA GREYDANUS

· · · ·

The one who eats everything must not treat with contempt the one who does not, and the one who does not eat everything must not judge the one who does, for God has accepted them. Who are you to judge someone else's servant? To their own master, servants stand or fall. And they will stand, for the Lord is able to make them stand.

Romans 14:3–4

How many of us have cooked a dish for someone that was received with some measure of disappointment?

Many of us have experienced that all-too-common scenario in which a parent carefully prepares a new recipe and places it in front of a skeptical child, where it is repeatedly poked at with a fork and eventually left uneaten on the plate. Maybe you have been that parent, and maybe at one time you were that child.

I'm not convinced, however, that we ever really outgrow this childish tendency toward criticism and dissatisfaction. Even as adults, we become disgruntled by situations we can't control, and where we can take control, we control too much.

I think about all the complex relationships my friends and family have with their food. Some of them control their diets to lose weight, gain muscle, lower their cholesterol, or develop more sustainable habits. Others manage special dietary restrictions due to food allergies, religious practices, or even addictions. Whether or not their reasons are wise and well-founded, their relationship with food has become a source of great anxiety.

I've noticed this fixation on food impacting our relationships with one another as well. One of my family members recently complained, "It's impossible to invite people over for dinner anymore. No one eats the same. I would have to cook a separate meal for each guest!"

I understand their frustration. Just like it is for the parent of a disapproving child, it is discouraging (and sometimes embarrassing) to prepare a meal for people who might not appreciate the effort. But as that conversation with my relative continued—and we grumbled about people's restrictive diets and how "they're practically forcing us to eat *their* way"—my own shortcomings became evident. There was a shameful lack of compassion in our words. We weren't just expressing frustration over the inconvenience of having to cook several dishes; we were being judgmental of the choices others had made regarding their eating.

As has always been the case, everyone has a unique understanding of the world, and we will make differing decisions when it comes to the food we eat. It is because of our own failings, like pride or insecurity, that we pass judgment on others. This pattern presents itself in all areas of our lives. We compare our choices with the choices of others in order to determine our value or success in life—whether we are comparing our jobs, our clothes, or even our food. In truth, God alone determines our value and success.

When it comes to our choices, it's important to remember that food, as with most things in this world, has the power to divide us—just as it has the power to bring us together. We can gather around the dinner table to either recognize our shared needs or emphasize each other's faults. So what do we do? How do we manage our differences in a manner that glorifies God?

Romans 14:3–4 reminds us that sharing a meal—and living in relationship with others—is not about why we have chosen to gather but rather the attitude in which we come. We are called to approach one another with humility. We are called to surrender our criticisms and focus on the greater reason why friends and family gather around the table, why we invite guests into our homes and provide nourishment for the ones we love. It is not to impress people with our cooking or even to satisfy our basic need for food. God calls us to the table to be in his presence and reflect the body of Christ. Despite our differences, we are all loved and accepted by the Lord, and that is a cause for pure, unburdened celebration.

May you come to the table today with a humble heart and take joy in what you have prepared—not because it is masterful or pleasing to others but because it was made in honor of the One we serve. And should anyone join your table with a hungering soul, may you bless them by your companionship and fill them with God's love.

CHICKEN DIVAN

Attributed to Rosalie Caldwell.

Serves 6

3 boneless skinless chicken breasts, diced (approx. 6½ cups)
3 broccoli heads (or 1 lb frozen broccoli florets)
1 (10.5 oz) can cream of chicken soup
⅓ cup mayonnaise
⅔ cup milk
1 tsp lemon juice
¾–1 cup grated cheddar cheese
4 Tbs butter, melted
1 cup bread or cracker crumbs

1. Preheat oven to 350°.

2. Sear or bake the chicken breasts until fully cooked. Set aside to cool.

3. If using fresh broccoli, cut the heads into florets and rinse. Bring a pot of water to boil over high heat, with enough water to submerge the broccoli. Once water is boiling, slowly add florets to the pot. Cook broccoli for 4–5 minutes or until tender. Drain broccoli and allow to cool.

4. Place cooked broccoli (or frozen broccoli) in a single layer in a 9×13 baking dish. Layer the diced, cooked chicken on top of the broccoli.

5. In a bowl, mix together cream of chicken soup, mayonnaise, milk, and lemon juice until thoroughly combined. Pour evenly over the chicken and broccoli. Then sprinkle grated cheese in an even layer on top.

6. Combine melted butter and bread or cracker crumbs in a separate bowl. Once the crumbs have soaked up a considerable amount of butter, spread the mixture evenly over the cheese.

7. Bake uncovered for approximately 30–40 minutes, or until the edges are golden brown and bubbling. Then remove from oven and let rest for a few minutes before cutting into squares. Best when served over rice.

The Sixth Love Language

BRIANNA DEWITT

· · · ·

And he took bread, gave thanks and broke it, and gave it to them, saying, "This is my body given for you; do this in remembrance of me." In the same way, after the supper he took the cup, saying, "This cup is the new covenant in my blood, which is poured out for you."

Luke 22:19–20

For most of my life, having a container of food on the counter from my grandma was a nearly everyday occurrence. It was often baked goods—cookies or Texas sheet cake or pumpkin bread—but sometimes it was chicken soup she had "made too much of" or lasagna that had "been in the freezer anyway." For a few months, while we made updates to a new-to-us house, my parents, two siblings, and I lived with my grandparents, and this food was part of our everyday lives at a different level than it had ever been before, much to my delight.

When I became an adult, I regularly invited myself over to my grandparents' house for, yes, free food, but also a few lively rounds of Rummikub, Five Crowns, or whatever other game we decided to play that night. I'd call once to pick a date, and then I'd often get a separate call back a few days later so we could discuss the menu. Eventually, I wised up and would have a good idea of what I wanted already in my head, since Grandma was going to ask anyway. My menu of choice was usually lasagna, cheesy bread, and a rotating selection of my favorite of Grandma's desserts.

The older I got, the more I realized how time-consuming her lasagna and cheesy bread were to make, yet I knew, without fail, she would happily make them for me, with Grandpa often pitching in as well. Sometimes we'd bake together, like making a large batch of oatmeal cookies that had to be iced while they were still warm and therefore necessitated at least two bakers. When I'd leave at the end of a night filled with stories and laughter, I'd need at least one bag—usually more—to carry the food I'd be sent home with.

One day, as I was reading about the concept of "five love languages," I realized there should be a sixth one, the one my grandma taught me: food. While food can certainly be tasty, when it's at its best I think it helps bring us closer to the people we love and even acts as a sign of that love. When someone is going through a difficult time, one of the first tangible things we often think to do is to bring them food. Certainly, it's a very practical need, but this act of service is also a way to care for people and express our love for them.

As I've realized how my grandma conveyed her love for us through food, I've begun to bring similar practices into my own life. It may come in the form of a labored-over birthday cake shaped like Winnie-the-Pooh for my nieces and nephews or a portion of soup for a family welcoming a new baby.

We see this connection between food and love suggested by Jesus himself, in the shape of the Last Supper. As he ate with his disciples for the last time before his death, he explained to them that the food was a demonstration of his love for them—his body, given for them, and his blood, shed for them. Jesus's death to save us was the ultimate act of love, and his comparison to food gives us a glimmer of what we might be able to convey to people through gifting or sharing food together.

The next time we receive a plate of cookies or give one away, let's remember that it's about far more than the food—it's about showing Jesus's love.

The International Table

RACHEL MCRAE

· · · ·

There is neither Jew nor Gentile, neither slave nor free, nor is there male and female,
for you are all one in Christ Jesus.

Galatians 3:28

Traveling across town or around the world can open us up to a wide variety of culinary delights. For people who consider themselves foodies and love to try a little bit of everything, the world is their smorgasbord. For people like me who admit to being picky eaters, it can be a bit daunting and not nearly the adventure it is for some of our traveling companions.

The first time I went to Poland, I stayed at a retreat center that served meals consisting of traditional Polish food. I recognized the occasional pork chop, carrot salad, and potatoes in their various forms. But for most of the week, I didn't know what I was looking at on my plate. Fish served with their heads still intact, shredded mystery meat in a gelatinous mound, cabbage stuffed with meat, and a variety of vegetables mixed in a variety of different sauces. That week turned into a weight loss program I had not anticipated.

But as my travels to Poland have continued over the years, my appreciation for and love of Polish food has grown. I now look forward to the bounty of soups, meats, vegetables, and desserts. Yes, I remain a picky eater, and there are things I still have not acquired a taste for (anything covered in a gelatinous mound, for example). But I realize the main change in my view of Polish cuisine is not the food itself but the people I share it with.

Those who were strangers to me on my first trip are now dear friends. We've shared many tables together in restaurants and cafés. We've partaken of randomly assembled lunches from the local gas station as we take a break from the work we've been doing. We've strolled cobblestone streets with scoops of lody (ice cream) in our hands as we discuss our lives, our interests, and our faith.

My favorite meals are those when we're invited into our friends' homes. We'll bring some meager dish we're able to whip together via a market stop on the way from where we're staying. It's a small contribution to what always ends up being a feast provided by our friends. Grilled kielbasa. Vegetables perfectly seasoned, many times fresh from their garden. Family recipes of pierogi and casseroles that have been made for who knows how many generations. An assortment of fruits and desserts always tops off the best meal I'll have all summer.

We sit around the table—enjoying the meal, yes, but more importantly, enjoying each other. I always take a moment during these gatherings to silently look around the table. It's a hodgepodge of people that, in human terms, should never know each other. We all live in different parts of the United States and in Poland. Some of us are Christians. Some are Jewish. Some have no faith. And yet, here we are. Only God can orchestrate a banquet and invitation like that.

The good news is that we don't have to travel thousands of miles from home to enjoy this kind of fellowship and amazing food. Next time you're having a meal, no matter how simple or how fancy, look around the table. Think about how good our God is to bring you together with those you are sitting with, whether it's two people or twenty. Appreciate all that they bring to your table and to your life. And be willing to try new friendships, new locations, and new dishes—you never know how they may all end up forever changing your life.

POLISH RASPBERRY CRUMBLE CAKE

Serves 9

For the cake

1 cup butter (2 sticks), room
   temperature
½ cup granulated sugar
4 lg eggs
1½ cups all-purpose flour

⅓ cup cornstarch
2 tsp baking powder
pinch salt
12 oz fresh raspberries

For the crumble topping

¼ cup cold butter (½ stick)
½ cup all-purpose flour

⅓ cup powdered sugar
pinch salt

1. Preheat oven to 350°. Beat softened butter with a mixer on high until fluffy (about 2–3 minutes). Add sugar and beat for an additional 3 minutes. Add eggs one at a time, and keep beating.

2. In a separate bowl, combine flour, cornstarch, baking powder, and salt. Add to the butter mixture by the spoonful. Mix until a smooth batter forms.

3. Line a 9×9 pan with parchment paper, and transfer the batter to the pan. Top with raspberries.

4. For the crumble topping, dice the cold butter and place in a medium-sized mixing bowl with flour, sugar, and salt. Massage with your fingertips until mixture resembles small curds (similar in size to cottage cheese). Top raspberries with crumble topping.

5. Bake for about 50–55 minutes, until golden brown on top.

A Gathering of Grateful Hearts

SHELLY SULFRIDGE

. . . .

My goal is that they may be encouraged in heart and united in love, so that they may have the full riches of complete understanding, in order that they may know the mystery of God, namely, Christ, in whom are hidden all the treasures of wisdom and knowledge.

Colossians 2:2–3

I grew up in the hills of Kentucky, where food was always a big part of our lives. I will never forget visits to Harlan County, where Daddy grew up. My grandparents moved often. Their homes were small but always welcoming. Their address may have been changeable but not the environment.

When we showed up, everyone else did too, and there were many of us. I come from a family of storytellers, and everyone talked at the same time. I could take my pick of which story to listen to. As conversations grew louder, aromas from the kitchen filled the house. The food was mouthwatering, made from scratch, and mostly harvested from the garden.

A typical meal included fresh vegetables: green beans, potatoes mashed with a big dollop of butter melting in the center, cucumbers, and tomatoes. The main attraction was the best fried chicken you've ever sunk your teeth into. It amazes me now that the chicken would sit out all night, and we would eat the leftovers for breakfast, and no one ever got sick.

Like the other dishes, the chicken was also homegrown. My aunt would walk out in the yard, chase down a chicken, and wring its neck. I don't even know how to convey this gently. She would swing the chicken around and around—and suddenly its neck would snap. She'd then walk over to a tree stump, take an axe, and chop its head off. When you hear the saying, "Don't mess with a Southern woman," remember this story.

My cousins and I would chase fireflies barefooted at night and then play church. My grandparents were part of a Pentecostal church. I remember us kids on the back porch playing church. We would sing, shout, and handle Papaw's belts like snakes—but if we saw a real snake, it scared the living daylights out of us. One night, my little cousin Lisa stepped into a JFG coffee can and stumbled off the porch. This porch was high off the ground, and I thought she'd killed herself, but she jumped up and kept right on shouting.

Before bedtime, the adults would tell scary stories. One night, after we went to bed, something fell off the dresser, and my sister and I woke everyone in the house with our screaming. Daddy came running into the room in his underwear, holding a shotgun. Mama said no more scary stories for us. Thank you, Mama.

The things that always remained constant in our family were stories, laughter or screams, good food, and faith. My family was far from perfect, but I'm thankful every day that I grew up knowing about Jesus. My parents and grandparents have gone on to heaven, and I look back on our visits with nostalgia and gratitude.

Bringing people together must be in my blood. We have two beautiful large tables my husband built. We can seat fourteen—or more, if needed. I love to see everyone talking, laughing, and eating together. These gatherings bring me joy, and although things are different, they make me think of family back in Kentucky.

I believe gathering together and filling our hearts and souls with laughter and good food brings glory to God, whether you are among family or not. God created us to be with other people. I'm an introvert, but I've learned I need the company of others for a healthy balance.

SHELLY'S SECRET SOUTHERN FRIED CHICKEN

Serves 6

1 chicken (cut up)
2 cups canola oil
salt and pepper

1½ cups buttermilk
2 cups flour
1 med onion, chopped

1. Heat two inches of canola oil in a large skillet (cast iron recommended) to around 350°.

3. Salt and pepper the chicken, dip each piece in buttermilk, and then roll in flour. Add the secret ingredient—onion—to the hot oil.

4. Add only four pieces of chicken to the pan at a time. Too many will make the chicken less crispy. The chicken needs to reach 165° before removing from the oil.

5. Remove the cooked chicken to a dish lined with paper towels for the grease to drain.

6. Repeat with remaining chicken pieces. This can be a messy, tiring process, so allow yourself and the chicken time to rest before eating.

Note: If you have time, you can marinate the chicken in buttermilk for several hours (or overnight) to help tenderize the chicken.

Celebrate Lavishly

KRISTEN D. FARRELL

. . . .

On this mountain the Lord Almighty will prepare a feast of rich food for all peoples, a banquet of aged wine—the best of meats and the finest of wines . . . he will swallow up death forever. The Sovereign Lord will wipe away the tears from all faces; he will remove his people's disgrace from all the earth. The Lord has spoken.

Isaiah 25:6, 8

I love food. I love making food, thinking about food, shopping for food, preparing food, and hosting people to share meals with. And I am a pretty good cook too, which has worked to my family's advantage—*mostly*. Sometimes we have a hard time deciphering food for just plain old sustenance (food as fuel) and the *experience* food can give us when it is more than a meal—when it's a feast—a banquet. Recently, my husband and I heard about a restaurant in our hometown of Buffalo that had been nominated for a James Beard Award. Born in 1903, James Beard was an American chef, cookbook author, teacher, and television personality. He pioneered television cooking shows, taught at the James Beard Cooking School in New York City and in Oregon, and lectured to wide audiences. He was hands down one of the original foodies before foodies were even a thing and before we had television networks devoted to food. Beard taught and mentored generations of professional chefs and food enthusiasts and published more than twenty books.

Where am I going with this? Give me one more second. Beard was quoted as saying, "Like the theater, offering food and hospitality to people is a matter of showmanship, and no matter how simple the performance, unless you do it well, with love and originality, you have a flop on your hands."*

* James Beard, *Delights and Prejudices* (New York: Open Road Media, 2015), 212.

All this to say—there is a difference between a meal and a feast, a meal and a banquet. And if you've roamed through the Scriptures, Old and New Testaments alike, you've noticed that food shows up in metaphors, parables, and analogies. When it comes to banquets, if fancy food isn't your thing, think of the difference between an overly processed deli turkey sandwich on soggy white bread with wilted lettuce versus a Thanksgiving feast. One is just food—the other a matter of showmanship!

I love this as it connects with the picture Isaiah paints of a banquet, a feast of celebration. Carefully selected foods—cheeses from a boutique market with good drinks—earning a James Beard award or a Michelin star. And it will be this lavish banquet that preludes the ultimate joy of God's people—the swallowing up of death and the wiping away of all tears that Isaiah writes about.

So much joy—so much to celebrate—the waiting is over! And these types of feasts show up in lots of places in Scripture, ritual banquets that marked some personal or interpersonal transition or transformation, held to give honor to those undergoing important social change. In other words, food isn't just fuel. Food means something bigger than itself. A way to connect. A way to celebrate. A way to give and exchange love and care. Might I even suggest a way to have fun?

The business of faith is serious, no doubt, but sometimes Christians can be wet blankets. If it's not somber enough, it's not spiritual enough. If it's not practical, it must not be reverent enough. But, hey, when was a lavish meal ever practical? As followers of Christ, we can have both a thoughtful, God-honoring faith and a faith that should include *fun*. Joy. And some serious celebrations.

To know that is the mystery of our faith and the mystery of a Savior who loves us enough to die for us *and* invites everyone to the greatest feast ever. As with all invites, we can only experience the goodness if we show up—really show up—and understand the invitation that's been given. This isn't an invitation for day-old pastries or a gas station hot dog. This is a *feast* with joy and love, a feast of freedom and abundance and award-winning hospitality. Let's respond as such.

The Connection of Family Comfort Food

BRIGGITTE P. BROWN

. . . .

*This is the bread that came down from heaven. Your ancestors ate manna and died,
but whoever feeds on this bread will live forever.*

John 6:58

Nothing gets the family to our dinner table faster than yelling, "The sancocho is ready!" It's a traditional stew made with meat and root vegetables, and it holds memories of love, connection, and satisfaction for our family. As a child, I watched my abuela, tias, and mami pour their hearts and souls into deep pots of sancocho. Their love and commitment were evident in the sizzling onions, celery, and peppers that patiently awaited the arrival of the beef and chicken. Root vegetables like yuca, pumpkin, yam, green plantains, and potatoes were diced and ready to jump into the pot. The amazing smells always greeted our senses as the stew would simmer until it was ready for us to feast.

The love that was put into the stew and shared around the family table on cold, rainy, or snowy nights was transformative. The connection to family and memories was strengthened every time sancocho was made. It was like a blanket of love that wrapped us up and healed every wound. Its warmth still reminds me of that family base and draws me back to those childhood memories.

As I grew older and had my own family, I learned that God also draws us. Love is even more satisfying when Jesus is our foundation. I continued the family tradition of cooking sancocho, and I taught my African American husband and our children about my Dominican roots. While the memories of comfort lingered in my soul, Jesus became my secret ingredient in the stew. As a little girl, I did not go to church and did not know about God. The comfort of connecting to food fell short of connecting us to the true soul healer. The true satisfaction of our full bellies. In our home now, with our seven children, God is our soul connection. The sancocho still draws us to the table of love, but God tugs our hearts and unites us in love. Food is how love was expressed through my past generations. It went beyond the small bowl of sancocho, arroz blanco, and slices of aguacate.

At times I cook with a heavy heart, filled with desires and prayers for my children's future. I mourn for the journey that my kids, adults themselves now, will need to walk and bear without me being the anchor of their strength. Now their base will hopefully also include Jesus. I think on my own journey and how I represented Christ for them. Did I do a good enough job modeling that relationship? Will this pot of love continue to draw their bellies back to our family table, to reconnect and enjoy the energy of our love? Have they learned to lean in closer to Jesus and our family base? I trust Jesus and release my fears to him. I know who he has been during our darkest times. God has always prevailed. Surely he will continue to prevail with our children.

Food has always been a unifying factor for families, but it can be transformative when Jesus is the foundation of our lives. The love that Jesus has poured into my heart and the areas he has healed fall into the pot as I cook and go into my family's bellies. They eat with such joy and excitement. They add their families to our table, and seeing the grandchildren feasting on Jesus's love and Mima's heart connects our family to the heart of Christ.

SANCOCHO
(MEAT STEW WITH ROOT VEGETABLES)

Serves 6–8

1 lb beef flank, chuck, or round, cut into small pieces

1 lb boneless chicken (dark meat preferred), cut into small pieces

juice of 2 limes

1 tsp minced fresh cilantro or parsley

½ tsp dried oregano

1 tsp minced garlic

1 tsp salt

4 Tbs vegetable oil

1 lb smoked turkey bones, cut into small pieces

2 ears corn, cut into ½-inch slices (optional)

2 beef bouillon cubes

2 chicken bouillon cubes

3 green (unripe) plantains, peeled and cut into 1-inch pieces

½ lb yuca (cassava), peeled and cut into 1-inch pieces

½ lb calabaza squash, diced

½ yam, diced

4 potatoes (Yukon gold or other yellow potato), diced

arroz blanco (white rice)

aguacate (avocado)

1. Place beef and chicken in a large bowl and season with lime juice, cilantro (or parsley), oregano, garlic, and salt. Marinate for at least half an hour; an hour is better.

2. In a large pot, heat oil over high heat. Add marinated meat and stir carefully. Cook, stirring, until meat is browned.

3. Add turkey bones and corn. Cook while stirring for a couple of minutes.

4. Lower heat to medium and pour 8 cups of water into the pot. Simmer until it breaks the boil.

5. Add beef and chicken bouillon cubes. Once the water returns to the boil, add the plantain and root vegetables (yuca, calabaza, yam, and potatoes).

6. Cover and simmer over low heat until vegetables are cooked through, about 45–60 minutes. It will thicken a bit while cooking. If it dries out too much, add water as necessary. Simmer uncovered to reduce if it is not thick enough for your taste.

7. Season with salt to taste. Remove from heat. Remove turkey bones, if desired, and serve. Sancocho can be enjoyed with a slice of avocado on the side and a bowl of white rice.

Hand upon Hand

TAMMY GERHARD

· · · ·

Follow my example, as I follow the example of Christ. I praise you for remembering me in everything and for holding to the traditions just as I passed them on to you.

1 Corinthians 11:1–2

It was Cookie Day at my house—a more-than-fifteen-year tradition of inviting the young women I mentor to come together at my home to bake cookies and share stories the Saturday before Christmas. Five women gathered, hand upon hand, pressing cookie cutters into flattened dough in the middle of a floured table. As the cookie cutters were poised to make their impressions, I was reminded of the impression my own mentor had made on my life many years ago.

I was a young mom, and my daughter had just turned three. I had recently discovered I was pregnant again, and my hormones were causing mean bouts of nausea. I was overwhelmed but did not know where to turn. That is when Mrs. Brown stepped into my life.

I met her at our church on Mother's Day. We had moved from another state and, as it turned out, she had lived in that state as well. That fact made for an immediate connection. Before I even realized how much I needed it, Mrs. Brown was coming over regularly, playing with my daughter, and allowing me the time and space to enjoy a warm meal, a little rest, and a shower in the midst of the unexpected struggles of my pregnancy. When so many would run away from the messy places in people's lives, Mrs. Brown ran toward them and brought the love of Jesus with her.

In the last month of my pregnancy, I came downstairs from a nap and found Mrs. Brown, hand upon hand with my little girl, making Christmas cookies. The delicate dough formed angels and stars as they carefully used the cookie cutters and then decorated the freshly baked and cooled cookies with delicious homemade icing. Out of the corner of her eye, she saw me walk in and called me over to take her place. Now I, hand upon hand with my girl, was pressing the cutter into the cookie dough, receiving from Mrs. Brown the tradition that would last well into my future and touch the lives of not just my daughter but numerous young women I mentored over the years.

Just like those cookie cutters imprinted into the dough, Mrs. Brown left an imprint on my life. As she spent time with me, she shared stories of raising her family and how her faith informed her decisions. She read the Bible with me and prayed with me. My life was sweeter in so many ways because she moved toward a messy young mama with acts and words of love and grace. She reflected Jesus and left her mark on my life because he had made his mark on hers.

Sometimes God brings a special person into our lives to help us get to know him better. That individual helps us grow to understand Jesus more because the way they engage with us reflects the God they love. Can you think of individuals who have been part of your life in that way? What traditions have you encountered, and even passed on to others, because of their investment in you?

If you have been given this gift, ask Jesus who he might want you to pass it on to. Pray for that person now, inviting Jesus to move through you. What are ways you might share God's love with this person? Choose one of these and do it today, trusting that God will make a lasting mark of his love on their life through you!

MRS. BROWN'S SUGAR COOKIES AND BUTTERY DECORATOR ICING

Yields 3 dozen cookies

Dry ingredients

3 cups flour
1 cup butter (2 sticks), softened, or shortening

1 tsp baking soda
2 tsp baking powder
¼ tsp salt

Wet ingredients

2 eggs
1 cup sugar

½ tsp vanilla
¼ cup milk

1. Preheat oven to 350°.

2. In a bowl, combine all dry ingredients with a fork until fully mixed, and put aside.

3. In a separate bowl, combine all wet ingredients. Add to dry ingredients, mixing until dough forms a ball. If the dough seems too sticky to roll and cut, add a sprinkle or two of flour to the mixture.

4. Wrap dough in plastic wrap and refrigerate for one hour.

5. Remove chilled dough ball from the plastic wrap and place on a well-floured surface. Using a flour-covered roller, roll out the dough until it is ¼ to ½ inch thick, or to your liking.

6. Use your favorite cookie cutters to cut out the dough. Place on parchment paper–covered cookie sheets with room between them, and place into hot oven. Bake for 8–10 minutes, until lightly browned on bottom.

Decorator Icing

½ cup butter (1 stick), softened
¼ cup shortening
1 tsp vanilla

¼ tsp salt
4 cups powdered sugar
2–4 Tbs milk

1. In a large bowl, beat butter and shortening until creamy. Add vanilla and salt.

2. Slowly mix in powdered sugar and milk, alternating, until you reach your desired consistency.

3. You may choose to separate icing into containers to add your choice of food coloring.

4. Using either a knife to spread or a piping bag to add details, frost your cooled cookies. (Add sprinkles for a festive touch!)

Feeding the Growth

AMY BALLOR

· · · ·

There is a time for everything, and a season for every activity under the heavens . . .
a time to weep and a time to laugh, a time to mourn and a time to dance.

Ecclesiastes 3:1, 4

A mama's first job is always to feed her child. From the moment I saw those two pink lines, I loaded my belly full of cottage cheese, all the green veggies, and any chocolate-covered peanut butter I could find (for balance, of course).

Then that little one greeted the world with a hearty scream, and I thanked God for this tiny miracle. I happily nursed him from my breast and watched his arms grow fat little rolls and his belly stretch into a healthy mound over his diaper.

As he grew, the infant and toddler years were a treat at the dining table. When I wasn't pulling spaghetti out of his ginger locks or scolding him for feeding our cockapoo, I was mashing creamy avocado onto toast and sneaking sweet potato into homemade mac and cheese for some extra vitamin C.

I was doing good, feeding my growing boy. We had an understanding. I only wanted him to be strong and healthy. And he gobbled up most things I set before him. Except black beans, of course. Or pinto beans. Or anything bean shaped. Those taste like dirt, ya know.

And then he got old enough to pull up a chair to stand on and stir the ground turkey on Taco Tuesday, the sharp dust of cumin making our mouths water. We would laugh as he mixed the flour for Saturday morning pancakes and danced to "Down by the Bay" as the bacon sizzled.

Soon his legs grew longer and leaner, and he no longer required a chair to reach the counter. His need for a filling breakfast turned into the need for a second breakfast, then a snack, then lunch, then another snack, dinner, then a bedtime snack while he devoured the latest Harry Potter book in the dwindling daylight. My footprints became permanently molded into the flooring where I prepared meal after meal. I was doing good, feeding my growing boy.

Then it happened—slowly at first. Our lives became busier with more children and school and sports and friends. Instead of sidling up next to me to peel potatoes, he was spending the night with buddies and walking up to the gas station for Reese's Peanut Butter Cups and Mountain Dew slushies . . . and meeting girls. "Can I just eat when I get home?" he'd ask. "Sure, I'll make a plate for you," I'd promise. And I did. Then he got wheels, and the freedom sixteen had to offer meant he'd stay for dinner (rushing through the meal and the small talk) but be gone until just a minute or two after curfew. I was always thankful for the short time we had to say grace and catch up.

But these days, things are different. I now have a little more time and experiment with new recipes. And he's met a special girl. A sweet girl whom I adore and he doesn't want to go one moment without. Now he's off sometimes all day, embracing work and love and everything it means to come of age. Still, I flutter about the stovetop restlessly but with purpose, checking my phone for a text about whether or not I should count him in for dinner. It's tuna casserole night, his favorite. "YES! I'll be there," he writes. So I sauté and stir and scrape, aiming for perfection like I truly have chef's hands.

And after dinner, when he sidles up next to his girlfriend at the stove to bake cookies, I realize I did good. I fed my boy and now he's grown. This was God's plan. I may cry because life goes by so quickly, but my heart is full of the sweetest memories.

The seasons will always change. And although we might not always be ready for it, we can trust that God is by our side through it all.

He's there in our tears. And he's there smiling with us when we smile. Whether we're launching our kids from the nest or saying our final goodbyes to a beloved parent or moving on from an unhealthy relationship, it's okay to embrace all our feelings. It helps us grow. And remember: God has given us even this season for a purpose.

Extraordinary Abundance

COURTNEY ZONNEFELD

. . . .

Why are you talking about having no bread? Do you still not see or understand? Are your hearts hardened?

Mark 8:17

Every November, I look forward to the day before Thanksgiving almost more than I look forward to the holiday itself. American Thanksgiving always falls on a Thursday, and so that Wednesday is always full of preparation. When I had to drive to Iowa for the holiday, I'd make sure to arrive by Tuesday night so that Baking Day (as my mother and I call it) could start as early as possible.

When God leads his people out of Egypt, he promises them a "land flowing with milk and honey" (Exod. 3:17). To the ancient Israelites, milk and honey would not have been everyday oatmeal toppings; they were signs of an abundance these former slaves had never known. And when manna falls for them in the years before reaching the promised land, that bread from heaven will also taste like honey.

Feeding ourselves does not have to be joyful; oftentimes, it is drudgery or just necessity. But every once in a while, a celebration can shock us out of our normal routines. Maybe this is why God sets up cycles of feasting for his people in Exodus: sometimes we need to celebrate not because we feel like it but because God's goodness is steady, regular, and unchanged by time.

When I plan holiday meals, I also plan for an abundance. Celebrations make me want to have far more than enough. I long to fill a table with a main dish and seven sides, to make everyone's favorites and maybe a few new recipes as well. I want enough pie to have a slice this afternoon, tonight, and tomorrow, and enough stuffing to nibble into December. I want enough loaves of bread to bring to Friendsgivings and the people next door.

On Baking Day morning, I wake up early and head to my parents' kitchen in my pajamas. The family cat shadows me as I gather ingredients. Baking Day always begins with bread: the same potato bread recipe my mother grew up making in the same bowl we use each year. The recipe requires three rises, and so I begin the day with yeast and water and potato flakes. I cover the dough in a tea towel, shower the flour out of my hair, and then return to the kitchen to dust myself with flour all over again.

When Jesus feeds the four thousand, he starts with seven loaves of bread, and the meal ends with seven baskets of leftovers. A little later on, his disciples begin to panic about their single loaf of bread when Jesus asks them: "And don't you remember? . . . [H]ow many basketfuls of pieces did you pick up? . . . Do you still not understand?" (Mark 8:18–19, 21). Peter, James, John, and the rest had forgotten not only what they had seen but also that they were traveling with a God who provides not only enough but beyond what we ask or imagine.

As Baking Day continues, my mother and I dance around each other in the kitchen, sometimes assisting or tasting each other's recipes. My father and sister dart in and out, stealing bites of dough and stuffing. Some years, after the dishes are washed, we wait for guests, friends, or acquaintances to arrive. Others, we watch the clock, ready to leave with basketfuls for a gathering.

On Thanksgiving Thursday, faces familiar and new gather around the table. We devour scoops of stuffing and slather honey butter on potato bread. We share stories of gratitude, and we remember those missing because of distance or loss. And we celebrate—not always because we feel like it, but because it is time.

THANKSGIVING POTATO BREAD AND HONEY BUTTER

Yields 9 loaves

5 cups lukewarm water
½ cup shortening
 (I like butter-flavored)

3½ Tbs salt
¾ cup instant potato buds

1. Mix these ingredients together in a large glass bowl with a spout. Let cool.
2. Then mix the following ingredients in an even larger bowl:

1 cup lukewarm water
½ cup sugar

4½ tsp yeast (2 packets)
10–12 cups all-purpose flour (start with 10)

3. Once the ingredients are combined, add cooled potato mixture. Mix well. Add flour till dough is of handling consistency. Knead for 8–10 minutes. Cover and let rise until double. Knead again for 2–3 minutes. Let rise until double once again.

4. Form loaves and place in pans; if using traditional 9×5 loaf pans, you'll need about nine. At this stage, you can choose to form the dough into other types of rolls or braids.

5. Arrange loaves on every available open surface (tables, countertops, the top of the oven, etc.) and let rise until double one more time.

6. Bake at 375° for 30–40 minutes, or until golden brown. Decrease time by 5–10 minutes if making rolls or other smaller shapes. Remove from oven and let cool. Serve with honey butter.

Honey Butter

1 cup honey, preferably local
1 cup sugar

1 cup heavy whipping cream

1. Combine all ingredients in a saucepan. Heat and stir until boiling. Boil for only 1 minute.
2. Remove from heat and add:

dash salt
1 tsp vanilla extract

1 lb unsalted butter (4 sticks), melted

3. Process mixture in blender until blended together. Transfer to containers and refrigerate. Slather on bread.

The Habit of Gathering

KIMBERLY LEONARD

· · · ·

And let us consider how we may spur one another on toward love and good deeds,
not giving up meeting together, as some are in the habit of doing, but encouraging
one another—and all the more as you see the Day approaching.

Hebrews 10:24–25

O ur family loves the Lord of the Rings movies. There is a dinner scene
in *The Hobbit* where plates are flying and mugs are filled, and there is
music and laughter to go around. It looks like chaos, but it also looks like our
family dinner table on Sunday nights. We began a tradition many years ago
to start the week off with a table surrounded with family, friends who have
become family, and any brave soul who cares to join. Part of the allure of these
Sunday night gatherings is the infamous dinner question that comes along
with the meal. The question varies to include topics like "What would you
title the autobiography of your life, and why?" or "Would you rather meet
one elephant-sized duck or one hundred duck-sized elephants, and why?" to
name a few. The question always includes "And why?" because this is where
the individual gets to share the reasoning for their answer and, in the process,
share something of themselves. The laughter, debate, and appreciation that
ensue around our dinner table over these shared answers join us together,
and we start the week off connected and encouraged.

I think there is a pressure to fill our weekends so full that we start our
week on empty. I know that has certainly been true for our family. Although
I would love to say I had this great idea to bring our family together, these
Sunday night dinners began almost by accident. It was a move to a new house
that opened an opportunity to sit in our new dining room, and I randomly

asked a silly question one night. Our boys loved it, and we laughed and lingered around our table long after the meal was done. The next weekend the boys asked for more silly questions, and that was how our weekly Sunday night dinner with silly questions was born. It became something we all looked forward to. Sometimes we were elbow to elbow because many joined us, and other times it was just a couple of us. No matter the number, it was about connecting, laughing, and being together.

Hebrews 10:24–25 reminds us that there is value in developing the habit of meeting with one another for the purpose of encouragement. It also describes an intentionality, as the author shares, "Let us consider how . . ." When I read this, I believe we have a sincere desire to form deep relationships with our family and friends, but sometimes we are not sure how to orchestrate it because we get caught up in the *how* and forget *why* we want to connect in the first place.

Our family loves to eat, enjoys laughing, and needs the extra time before the busyness of the week starts to be together, and the dinner table on Sunday night creates the setting for our connecting. How about your family? What if you consider some of the natural times you gather and build on these moments to "spur one another on"?

No matter how busy our schedules can get, there is great value in taking advantage of creating a time to gather together. It does not have to look like the crazy *Hobbit* dinner scene with plates flying, and it is not even about the actual food on the table. Instead, it is finding the "And why?" of those we meet as we get to know one another, encourage one another, and spur on one another.

Beautiful, Flavorful Variety

KATIE M. REID

. . . .

O Lord, what a variety of things you have made! In wisdom you have made them all. The earth is full of your creatures.

Psalm 104:24 NLT

My friend Suha is originally from the Middle East. When she moved to Canada, she attended a French culinary school. One time she asked me to do a photo shoot for her family with my nice camera, and she paid me in savory Arabic food. I think I got the better end of the deal—it was delicious!

When Suha heard my tween daughter was trying out for a popular TV cooking competition for kids, she offered to give her some lessons. She introduced my daughter to Arabic spices like sumac, which is a deep red color and gives food a tartness like lemon juice does. It was fascinating to learn about—and *smell*—the variety of spices she uses to season her chicken, like cumin, cardamom, ground cloves, nutmeg, coriander, allspice, and cinnamon.

Suha and I speak with different accents, wear varying styles of clothes, and cook with distinct blends of spices—there is so much variety in God's creation. And that's a good thing! When we expand our palate to try new dishes or interact with people who talk, look, and cook differently than we do, we experience a taste of what heaven will be like.

Revelation 7:9–10 reads:

After this I looked, and behold, a great multitude that no one could number, from every nation, from all tribes and peoples and languages, standing before the throne and before the Lamb, clothed in white robes, with palm branches in their hands, and crying out with a loud voice, "Salvation belongs to our God who sits on the throne, and to the Lamb!" (ESV)

Not only has God created variety in the plants, animals, and humans he has made but he welcomes into heaven those from all tribes, peoples, and languages who put their trust in his Son, Jesus, as their Savior and Lord. In other words, there is a big table ready to receive all those who choose, by faith, to believe in Jesus and accept his sacrifice for their sin upon the cross (see 1 John 1). Any of his children, from anywhere, whether the Middle East or the Midwest, can experience the unconditional love of Father God, on earth as it is in heaven.

My daughter tried out for the cooking show and made it past the first round of auditions. In the holding room at the audition venue, there were kid cooks from all over. The room housed a variety of God's creation, and it was a beautiful thing to behold. My daughter didn't go on to the next round, but she now carries the skills she gleaned from Suha's cooking lessons with her, and I do too. Trying new things, even when it is out of our comfort zone, and appreciating the variety of spices, experiences, and people God has created makes the world more beautiful and flavorful. And it's a taste of what's to come.

SUHA'S SEVEN-SPICE CHICKEN

Recipe from Suha Thiab.

Serves 2–4

1 med yellow onion, sliced
1–2 Tbs unsalted butter
1 lb boneless chicken thighs, diced
1 tsp ground cumin
1 tsp ground cardamom
1 tsp ground cloves

1 tsp ground nutmeg
1 tsp ground coriander
1 tsp ground allspice
1 tsp ground cinnamon
1 tsp ground sumac
salt and pepper to taste, if desired

1. Cook onion in butter for 5–8 minutes on low heat in a sauté pan.

2. Add chicken pieces and turn up to medium-high heat. Add all spices except the sumac and stir.

3. Cook chicken about 10 minutes, until done. Add the sumac and cook 1–2 minutes more. Serve with rice or naan or in a pita.

Kitchen Kingdom

KRISTEN D. FARRELL

· · · ·

For where two or three gather in my name, there am I with them.
Matthew 18:20

Everyone has their COVID story. Many are painful and wrought with sorrow, or at the very least wrought with frustration and grief. My family, like most, tried to make the best of a more than inconvenient situation and were fortunate to escape the tragedy that many experienced through indefinite job layoffs, the stress of frontline employment, or a terminally ill loved one.

My family of five packed up and headed north with my seventy-six-year-old mom to meet up with my sister and her family. Our destination: our shared second home in the south-central Adirondacks. Eleven of us quarantined together, enjoying fellowship and some of the COVID freedoms that summer allowed: time at the sun-drenched and eerily empty beach, vigorous hikes after being cooped up, the joy of togetherness and connection, and lots and lots of cooking.

Once a week, my sister and I would meal plan as we drove the winding mountain roads to our "local" grocery store an hour and a half away. We would talk or not, listen to music or not. But one thing never changed: the two of us companioning together to feed our families. It wasn't a task for the faint of heart, and we are not a cereal-for-breakfast family. Let me put it this way: if each person had two eggs every morning, four days a week, we'd need to buy, pack, and transport eight dozen eggs. It was a lot.

We realized, as we cooked together, that we were better together. Some nights, making dinner felt like an intricately choreographed and rehearsed masterful dance of detail and productivity. Other times, I'd stand in front of the finger-smudged stainless steel refrigerator and insecurely ask her, "What did you want?" like an absent-minded preteen at a middle school dance.

Years later, that is my most dominant memory of the pandemic. The food we produced could rival most five-star restaurants; we really are good cooks, but that isn't what I'm talking about. What I am talking about is the beauty of belonging. The power of connection. The goodness of grace. The sacredness of sisterhood.

There is a reason Jesus promises his presence specifically when we gather together. Ultimately, we are hardwired for community. We aren't called to go it alone. Introverts or extroverts, we need fellow travelers to enrich and develop our faith. Of course, we grow in our faith in solitude too, experiencing God's presence while quietly viewing a pink sunset as the bright orange fades into soft pastels. But more times than not, enjoying the presence of God through relationships makes the intangible tangible and his love and provision evident. The shared belly laughter of being together at our small community group of irreverent Christ-followers ushers in abundant joy. When I exchange a knowing glance with my husband at a subpar fourth-grade band concert where squeaky saxophones steal the show, I understand faithful commitment. And being in the kitchen with my older sister and a pasta pot boiling over with steamy water, I glimpse the undeserved love and presence of a Savior who died for me. He is with us and among us in these sacred relationships, if only we have the eyes to see.

SISTERS' SIGNATURE CAESAR

Serves 4

½ red onion, thinly sliced
¼ cup red wine vinegar
3 romaine hearts
salt and pepper to taste
2 Tbs rough chopped fresh dill, divided

½ cup shredded Parmesan, divided
good quality Caesar dressing (like Brianna's)
3 hard-boiled eggs, peeled
3 slices cooked bacon

1. Marinate the thinly sliced red onion in vinegar for 20 minutes to make pickled onions.

2. Wash and rip romaine, then give it ample time to dry or use a salad spinner. This helps avoid a soggy salad. Place lettuce in a large bowl and sprinkle with salt and pepper, half of the fresh dill, and half of the Parmesan. Add dressing and toss until ingredients are well blended and lettuce is evenly coated.

3. Top with remaining Parmesan, pickled red onion, crumbled bacon, and sliced or diced egg. Add additional dill for garnish.

The Story of Food

BRIANNA DEWITT

. . . .

And he directed the people to sit down on the grass. Taking the five loaves and the two fish and looking up to heaven, he gave thanks and broke the loaves. Then he gave them to the disciples, and the disciples gave them to the people.

Matthew 14:19

When I'm meeting a new person or trying to facilitate a conversation with a group of people who may not know each other well, one question I like to ask is, "What's the story of one of your favorite meals?" I'm quick to clarify it doesn't have to be one the person made themselves (though it certainly could be) or even something fancy—it's about the *story* of the meal, not just the food itself.

A meal from a vacation is a pretty common answer, and the first meals that pop into my head are usually times when I've been away from home as well—maybe because we're often more relaxed on vacation, or more likely to try a restaurant we don't have near us, or have a little extra time to make a new dish. As I think more deeply, though, other meals start to surface in my mind. It might be a particularly heartfelt holiday moment, a long-labored-over recipe, or just the right food at just the right moment that sticks out to me in a special way.

This question about the story of a favorite meal gets at something deeper too. Sure, I like hearing about the food itself and why the person loved it (and perhaps where I can find the recipe), but one of the aspects of food I appreciate is that it does much more than fill us up and give us energy. When God was designing humans, he didn't *have* to make it so we have to eat, and he certainly didn't have to make food taste so good or give us endless ways to combine edible items to create new ways of experiencing flavors. But food brings people together, encourages creativity as we incorporate it into meals, and gives us something to gather around at the table. All of these put together helps us both create and remember beautiful moments in life.

In reading through the Gospels, it's interesting to note how many times food is mentioned or even involved in one of Jesus's miracles. His very first miracle, as recorded in John 2, takes place at a wedding banquet. He helps the couple celebrate this big life moment by making sure they don't run out of wine for their guests, kicking off his earthly ministry. More than once, Jesus multiplies food so that those who have gathered to hear him won't go away hungry. And at his last meal with his disciples, he compares bread to his body that would be given for them, and wine to the blood he would spill for them. It makes me wonder how Jesus's followers would have answered when asked about the story of their favorite meal.

Certainly Jesus and all his followers had to eat for sustenance, as all humans do, but Jesus also shows some of the ways food can be so much more than practical. While we're unlikely to perform any food-specific miracles (though sometimes things taste so good it might *feel* like a miracle), we can see Jesus's examples of using food in his ministry as a path for ways we can use food in our lives as well. We may be able to help others celebrate by bringing food to a gathering or making extra effort to provide something special for an everyday occasion. We may be able to help provide for people who need it, perhaps by volunteering at a food pantry or dropping off a meal to those going through a difficult time. Or maybe we can share a story of a special meal, and then give thanks to the God who allows us to appreciate it.

The Fragrance of Family

MAGGIE WALLEM ROWE

. . . .

Then she gave Jacob the delicious meal, including freshly baked bread.
Genesis 27:17 NLT

When God makes it clear that you are to raise someone else's children in addition to your own, it shouldn't be that difficult, correct? You're already immersed in parenting—how hard could it be to add a couple more kids to the mix?

Some years ago, a pair of preteen siblings who had once lived in our neighborhood suddenly needed a home. At the time, our own three children were also preteens. When no relatives came forward to take in the brother and sister, who would almost certainly be separated in the foster care system, my pastor-husband and I knew that caring for these children was God's assignment for us.

While sobered by the responsibility, we were confident that God would provide what we needed for our newly blended family of seven. Our heavenly Father would ensure we could clothe their bodies, fill their bellies, and provide the love and protection they deserved.

One key ingredient was missing from the fresh stew of people in our home, however: communication. Our new children had endured years of trauma before the authorities placed them with us. They met our questions about their school day, food preferences, and personal needs with awkward silence. Even though our biological children tried to engage their new siblings in conversation, the atmosphere in our home quickly became strained. How could we get them to open up?

Keeping five hungry kids fed meant multiple trips to the grocery store each week, and even then a gallon of milk or loaf of bread didn't last a day. In desperation, I pulled out my bread machine one evening after supper. As I poured in milk and added honey and molasses, I prayed about the children's reticence that seemed to be masking emotions they were unable to express. When I added wheat flour, oats, and yeast to the mix, I pleaded with God to show me how to see into the mind and heart of each of our children. Soon they would all be teenagers. If we couldn't reach them now, what hope did we have for the coming years?

With the baking cycle set for just over three hours, it was past nine o'clock when that first loaf emerged, filling our modest raised-ranch home with the fragrant scent of bread. As I set the loaf aside to cool, our new son emerged from behind his closed bedroom door.

"Is that bread saved for anything?" he inquired shyly.

While I had intended it for the next day's school lunches, I was thrilled he spoke up.

"It's for you!" I exclaimed, seizing a serrated knife. As I began to slice, another child emerged, drawn by the activity in the kitchen. Then another child came, and another. Soon all five kids were crowded around the kitchen table, crumbs falling to the floor as they slathered warm slices of bread with sweet butter. As they ate, they began to talk about their day. Not wanting to draw attention to how pleased we were, my husband and I stayed in the background, listening quietly to the chatter.

The next evening, I made bread again, followed by many evenings afterward. For the price of a few simple ingredients, God had given us a gift that could not be bought. Seven people were beginning to bond as a family unit around a shared experience—a love for bread.

HONEY WHOLE WHEAT BREAD

Yields 1 loaf

Place the following in bread machine

11 oz milk, warmed slightly

½ Tbs salt

3 Tbs honey

2 Tbs molasses

Add on top

3¼ cups combination of bread flour and wheat flour

1½ cups old-fashioned oats

2¼ tsp yeast (1 packet)

1. Use largest loaf (2 lb) cycle with dark crust option. Our machine cycle is just over 3 hours.

Feasting on the Word

Theology of the Garden

CECILIA BERKEMEIER

· · · ·

*I am the true vine, and my Father is the gardener. He cuts off every branch in me
that bears no fruit, while every branch that does bear fruit he prunes so that it will
be even more fruitful.*

John 15:1–2

I pause sometimes as I pass through the produce section. Seeing row after
row of uniform, perfectly misted vegetables, I am struck by a quiet moment of gratitude and wonder. It hasn't always been that way, but ever since
I began gardening, I haven't been able to look at the produce section in quite
the same way. As beautiful, ordered, and maybe even mundane as it is, I know
now that it tells only part of the story.

One of the first lessons in gardening is that vegetables don't grow on
pristine shelves, and they certainly don't come prewashed. They start as just
soil and seeds. Seeds that need to be tended, watered, guarded, cared for.
Soil that is, well, dirty. Full of worms and rocks and bits of sticks. And that's
just the beginning of the work. After the seeds sprout and begin to grow,
then comes the trimming, the staking and weeding, the tending and feeding.
Hours—often long, hot hours—are spent tending the plants that will become
the fruit that will become the harvest.

Gardening teaches us that growth happens in unseen, hidden ways. By the
time the first shoots break through the ground, the seed has already lived a
life of stretching and cracking, reaching toward the sun it can't yet see. As we
tend the land, we also become more aware of all the steps that come between
sowing and harvest. In everything we do, whether it's ordering a salad at a

restaurant or buying a bag of carrots at the store, we are participating in a line of hands that have tended the food that shows up on our tables and in our refrigerators.

The Lord reminds us in John's Gospel that he himself is the Gardener, the one who tends the seed and the soil of our souls. It's in the garden that he shows us the ways that this dirty, steady, sweaty work is not unlike the work he does in our hearts.

Sometimes in life, it can feel as if we're putting in so much effort and not seeing any results. In these moments, I'm reminded of seeds, of growth that happens underground, unseen. I'm reminded that before the fruit there are leaves, and before leaves there are roots, and before roots there is just a seed, waiting quietly, preparing for the moment when the warmth and subtle changes of its surroundings invite it to come forth, invite it to do the thing it was created to do all along.

Our Gardener—the One who tends us, who brings us to life—invites us to participate in this gentle and steady work. In the everyday miracle of seeds, he proves to us that life can come from death and that the work—even quiet, unseen work—is never wasted.

Since gardening, I pause more in the grocery store. I pause more at dinner tables. Sometimes I take a moment and let myself be overwhelmed by the goodness of it all, by the awe and gratitude of the ordinary miracle of seeds becoming food.

HARVEST FOCACCIA

Inspired by Samin Nosrat's Ligurian focaccia. [*]
Yields 1 loaf

For the dough

2½ cups lukewarm water
½ tsp active dry yeast
2½ tsp honey
5⅓ cups all-purpose flour

2 Tbs kosher salt or 1 Tbs fine sea salt
¼ cup extra-virgin olive oil, plus more for
   pan and finishing
flaky salt for finishing

For the brine

1½ tsp kosher salt

⅓ cup lukewarm water

Toppings (pick whichever you like or whatever is in season)

sliced zucchini
fresh herbs
sliced tomatoes

sliced mushrooms
sliced onions

1. Stir together water, yeast, and honey to dissolve. Add flour, salt, and olive oil, and mix it all together. Cover dough and leave out at room temperature for 12–14 hours, or until double in volume.

2. Generously oil a rimmed baking sheet (an 18×13 sheet pan works well) and dump out the dough onto it. Gently stretch dough out over the pan and drizzle some more olive oil on top. Let rest for 30 more minutes, then dimple dough with your fingers. Make the brine by mixing salt and water, then pour it out over the dough to fill in the dimples. Let sit for 45 more minutes, until dough is light and bubbly.

3. Preheat oven to 450°.

4. At this point, you can either bake the bread as is or decorate with herbs and sliced vegetables.

5. Bake for 25–30 minutes or until golden brown. (It will take a bit longer if you've added toppings.)

6. Remove from the oven and drizzle a bit more olive oil on top while the bread is still hot. You can store it in an airtight container, but it's best enjoyed warm!

* Samin Nosrat, "Ligurian Focaccia," Salt Fat Acid Heat, accessed November 16, 2023, https://www.saltfatacidheat.com/fat/ligurian-focaccia.

An Everlasting Supply

REV. CATHERINE MILES

. . . .

I am the living bread that came down from heaven. Whoever eats this bread will live forever.

John 6:51

Bread is daily sustenance for life in many places around the world. When I was growing up, bread was part of almost every meal and one of our comfort foods. "Eat bread" is still a favorite family quote that reminds us of our childhood when other delicacies and staples were scarce at family meals. It was used as a supplement, satisfied our hunger, and gave us the nutrition we needed. At least, that is what we were taught and believed!

Even when God's people were suffering under Egyptian slavery, bread was an important food staple. After God delivered his people from slavery, manna was the "bread" he provided for the Israelites while they wandered in the desert. Each morning the families would collect the manna, and they would get double the amount on the sixth day so there would be enough for the Sabbath. "It was white like coriander seed and tasted like wafers made with honey" (Exod. 16:31). Wafers and honey may sound really tasty, but perhaps feasting on only one kind of bread while camping for forty years made it become mundane and unappreciated. (I don't think there was a cookbook on one hundred different ways to prepare manna.) Most of the Israelites became dissatisfied with the "same old, same old," and the joy of God's extraordinary provision became the agonizing consequences of a lifelong dry spiritual season.

The story of the Exodus is both exhilarating and excruciating. God provides food for the Israelites that is a miraculous demonstration of his glory. That is the exhilarating portion of the wilderness experience. The excruciating part is that the people complain to Moses and Aaron about their accommodations and food preferences, testing even God's patience. God hears their complaints, and in his mercy he chooses to "rain down bread from heaven" (v. 4). God provides in abundance, and the Israelites should have a delightful attitude of thanksgiving, but instead they have a grueling, long-term camping experience.

Jesus calls himself the Bread of Life that came from heaven. He refers to manna and the Exodus story when he says to the Jews, "Very truly I tell you, it is not Moses who has given you the bread from heaven, but it is my Father who gives you the true bread from heaven. For the bread of God is the bread that comes down from heaven and gives life to the world" (John 6:32–33). By missing this symbolism, the Jews of Jesus's day begin to question his message. They say, "Is this not Jesus, the son of Joseph, whose father and mother we know? How can he now say, 'I came down from heaven'?" (v. 42). The Jews only understand what they see in the physical realm, but Jesus is referring to the spiritual realm. He says he is the living bread that gives eternal life. The bread Jesus offers is from the Spirit and is the essential food for daily living. Abiding in him and living in him feeds and nourishes heart, soul, and body. It is not like the manna the Israelites ate, which only satisfied their physical needs, but is the bread that brings everlasting life to those who partake of it.

Spiritual hunger craves the things of God and can only be satisfied by the Bread of Life. The Israelites lost their spiritual hunger and became indifferent about the extraordinary works of God. This loss of appetite produced lives of discontent and disconnection with God. The consequences of their actions resulted in spiritual death.

God's desire is for all his children to feed on the Bread of Life and to never lose that spiritual hunger for the Word. Let us not become dissatisfied or disinterested in what Jesus offers us, for he reminds us that "whoever feeds on this bread will live forever" (v. 58). This bread is lifesaving and life-giving. Let the manna from heaven be your daily bread.

E-Z CINNAMON ROLLS

Yields approximately 2 dozen

4½ tsp yeast (2 packets)
½ cup warm water
½ cup sugar
¼ cup butter
2½ tsp salt
1½ cups hot water

2 eggs
6–7 cups bread flour or all-purpose flour
¼ cup butter, softened
¼ cup brown sugar
½–1 tsp cinnamon

1. In a small bowl, dissolve yeast in warm water. Set aside.

2. In a large bowl, combine sugar, butter, and salt. Add hot water, stirring until butter melts. Let cool for approximately 10 minutes. After mixture is cooled, add dissolved yeast and eggs to the bowl and whisk to combine.

3. Add flour, starting with 3 cups, and gradually add 3–4 cups more, as needed. Dough should be soft and pliable and easily formed into a ball.

4. Grease a large bowl, add the ball of dough, and cover with cloth or foil. Set in a warm place and let rise until double in size. Punch down to release air.

5. Grease two pie plates or 9-inch cake pans. Divide dough in half. Dust work surface with flour and roll out half of the dough with a rolling pin to approximately 12×8, until the dough is about ¼ inch thick, keeping edges as even as possible. Spread softened butter over dough, then sprinkle with brown sugar and cinnamon.

6. Roll the dough into a long tube similar to a jelly roll, starting on the longest side. Cut into 1-inch sections and place each roll in greased pan. Repeat with remaining half of dough and second pan. Cover and let rise again to double in size.

7. Bake at 350° for 12–15 minutes, until golden brown.

8. If desired, spread powdered sugar icing over warm rolls. Enjoy!

Feeding a Hungry Soul

ROBIN BUPP

. . . .

Man does not live by bread alone, but man lives by every word that comes from the mouth of the LORD.

Deuteronomy 8:3 ESV

What's the hungriest you've ever been? Racing off the bus at the end of each school day when I was young, I was certain it was impossible to be any hungrier than I was. I would head to my grandparents' house, where there was always a generous snack available, but on the best days there were fresh cookies. Whenever my uncle made a surprise visit, my grandfather would whip up a batch. They would still be warm when I arrived, and I'd stack up as many as I could carry from the counter, wondering aloud why—though these cookies were always appreciated—they tasted best immediately at the end of my school day. In his wise, quiet way, my grandfather would always remind me, "They taste best when you're hungry."

Many times in my life, I have had a hungry stomach; many times, I have had a famished soul.

I'm sure you have those seasons, too, when you feel like you're in a spiritual and emotional desert, and when you feel a lack inside that has nothing to do with your stomach. Maybe it's a relationship desert, or a desert of lost hopes and failed plans; sometimes I find myself in a desert of chaotic circumstances or even a financial desert. Sometimes I've wandered to these deserts through my own unwise choices, and other times they are just the circumstances that find me. However I've arrived, I find that my heart, and not my stomach, is off-the-bus-after-school hungry.

There are lots of things I can try to fill up on in these seasons, but I've been to these deserts enough times to see that God has a reason for my hunger. In the Bible, whenever God takes his people to the desert, he meets them there.

And you shall remember the whole way that the LORD your God has led you these forty years in the wilderness, that he might humble you, testing you to know what was in your heart, whether you would keep his commandments or not. And he humbled you and let you hunger and fed you with manna, which you did not know, nor did your fathers know, that he might make you know that man does not live by bread alone, but man lives by every word that comes from the mouth of the LORD. (Deut. 8:2–3 ESV)

The Israelites' situation created some very practical needs; in an actual desert, they lacked everything. But those material needs were just a signpost; the wilderness was an invitation to discover that the deepest needs in their hearts could be met regardless of their circumstances. Furthermore, the God who knows and heals hearts is also more than able to provide! He let his people hunger in the wilderness so they could discover his provision, know his care and goodness, and experience the sufficiency of his Word in every situation.

Whatever I may at first think I need when I find my soul is hungry, I've learned that—like the Israelites—this hunger is satisfied by God alone. Whatever relationships, circumstances, or needs I think I want God to take care of, his Word and presence in my empty soul are like my grandfather's cookies in my empty stomach: better because I'm hungry! He is always near, always my source—and yet, in my emptiness, I am so much more aware of his fullness.

GRANDPA GREEN'S COOKIES

Yields about 100 cookies

1 cup vegetable shortening or
   softened butter
¾ cup honey
¾ cup maple syrup
1 tsp vanilla
2 eggs

1½ cups flour
1 tsp baking soda
1 tsp salt
12 oz chocolate chips
1 cup chopped walnuts (optional)

1. Preheat oven to 350°.

2. Cream together shortening, honey, and maple syrup. Add vanilla and eggs and mix thoroughly. Slowly add flour, baking soda, and salt, mixing just until combined. (Dough is softer than average cookie dough.)

3. Stir in chocolate chips and walnuts, if using.

4. Drop by teaspoonfuls onto a greased cookie sheet. Bake for 10–12 minutes.

Consuming
without Savoring

OLIVIA PEITSCH

. . . .

But Martha was distracted by all the preparations that had to be made. She came to him and asked, "Lord, don't you care that my sister has left me to do the work by myself? Tell her to help me!" "Martha, Martha," the Lord answered, "you are worried and upset about many things, but few things are needed—or indeed only one. Mary has chosen what is better, and it will not be taken away from her."

Luke 10:40–42

My one-year-old daughter has the deepest passion for food I have ever seen. She has yet to meet a flavor, texture, or food scrap found on the floor that she doesn't like. We started her on a baby-led weaning path to allow her to have confidence in her eating and to help her explore a wide variety of flavors and textures. But there is one problem: I'm not convinced she is actually tasting anything.

If you are unfamiliar with baby-led weaning, the concept is simple: you cut finger-sized pieces of food small enough for a small child to grasp with their fists but large enough to not be a choking hazard. Well, these small, skinny pieces of food are the perfect size to go straight down her throat like it's a water slide. This girl will grab fistfuls of food at a time, packing it in until it's a soft enough mash to go down. Meanwhile, the rest of us hasten through our meal to try to appease her when she inevitably finishes first and demands more.

I'm not sure whether to be impressed or appalled. On the one hand, she is certainly getting exposed to a variety of foods, but on the other it seems a shame that she will eat a handful of Cheerios with as much gusto as home-made lasagna. She is being fed and she is growing, but the girl is missing out on the flavor and enjoyment that come with food.

What in your life have you been rushing through without *savoring*? For me, I hustle until I can rest, and I can't rest until everything is done. I fully identify with Martha when Jesus visits. She just wants her house to be clean for Jesus (I mean, come on, wouldn't we all?), but she has lost sight of what is important. In her frantic cleaning mode, she's missing out. She's consuming and not savoring.

Driving to work doesn't have to be time spent worrying about how messy my house is or mentally going through my to-do list. I can appreciate the breeze from the window or listen to that new podcast episode I've been putting off. Preparing dinner doesn't have to be a whirlwind; it can be a time to reflect, gather, and discuss. I can be thankful for a husband who loves to cook with me. I can cherish the peeks I get of my children playing together while they wait.

I know there are times in our lives we don't necessarily want to savor—illness, mourning, defeat—but in the midst of the loss and the heartache, we still have a constant. When we can't find the sweet moments, we can turn to our source of joy who created everything worth relishing. Seek God's goodness, and ask him to show you those glimpses of hope.

Despite the season you are in, time is fleeting. Whether you are urging time to speed up or desperately praying for it to slow down, it progresses at the same rate. But our good and gracious God has given us so much to be grateful for. No matter how messy life feels, may we be assured that God is still in control, still at work, and still offering us good gifts. Seek them out and cherish them.

Think about your moments of consumption. Are they simply feeding you, or are they *filling* you? See if you can identify a moment or activity you would identify as a feeding frenzy, and focus on what can be savored.

Soul Food

TYRA LANE-KINGSLAND

· · · ·

Beloved, I pray that you may prosper in all things and be in health, just as your soul prospers.

3 John 1:2 NKJV

Deeply rooted in the African American experience is soul food. Soul food is the rich ethnic food heritage of people of color in the United States. One of America's oldest cuisines, soul food was birthed out of the ingenuity of enslaved Black people drawing on their African traditions and using the meager rations they were given to create mouthwatering dishes that would be enjoyed for centuries to come.

Connecting us across miles and across the ages, soul food recipes weave a common thread and knit us together in bonds of mutual love and fellowship. From the hallowed halls of the White House to Grandma's house today, macaroni and cheese, collard greens, and candied yams have nourished our bodies and comforted our souls. And from your nana's tried-and-true banana pudding to your mother-in-law's famous potato salad, soul food recipes are enjoyed and passed down to bless and prosper those who partake of them.

Soul food is not merely nourishment for the physical body; it is sustenance for our souls. The soul of humankind is our minds, will, and emotions. When we commune with family and friends over beloved heirloom recipes, we have a unique opportunity to ease our minds, discern God's will, and soothe our emotions. Bringing together multiple generations and passing on traditions anchors the soul, rooting us in identity and belonging.

In today's verse, the writer prays we would prosper in all things. It calls to mind the abundance Jesus came to earth to give us. In John 10:10, Jesus tells us he came that we would have life and have it more abundantly. When we are grounded in the truth of who we are in Christ and in our family of origin through simple things like recipes, we have a solid foundation upon which we can grow. In this environment, recipes become more than a collection of ingredients; they serve as genealogy, telling the story of a people and leaving a legacy for those to come. And that sounds like a winning concoction for the soul for sure.

BLACK-EYED PEA AND COLLARD STEW

This recipe highlights two ingredients important to the African American experience. Black-eyed peas pay homage to African roots, and greens are a staple from north to south and east to west. This soulful, smoky dish is a satisfying one-pot meal. Pair with your favorite cornbread recipe, and you've got a dinner guaranteed to warm the heart and nourish the soul.

Serves 6

1 (14 oz) can diced tomatoes
4 lg cloves garlic, minced
1 chipotle pepper in adobo
¼ cup avocado or olive oil
1 lg onion, diced
1 med green bell pepper, deseeded and diced
1 tsp red pepper flakes

2 tsp chili powder
½ tsp smoked paprika
1 tsp sea salt
2 cups vegetable broth
1 bunch collard greens, washed, stemmed, and chopped
2 cups cooked black-eyed peas

1. Blend tomatoes, garlic, and chipotle pepper in a blender until smooth. (If you want less heat, first remove the seeds from the chipotle pepper.)

2. Heat oil over medium heat in a large pot. Add onions and green pepper and sauté for 5–7 minutes, until tender.

3. Add tomato mixture and all spices and simmer for 5 minutes. Add broth and collards and cook over medium heat for 15 minutes. Add black-eyed peas and cook for an additional 10 minutes, until flavors combine.

Homemade Bread and the Bread of Life

MARLA DARIUS

. . . .

For we are to God the pleasing aroma of Christ among those who are being saved and those who are perishing.

2 Corinthians 2:15

Smells and aromas often evoke memories and bring us back to a place and time we once were.

My mom is an excellent bread baker, and growing up we often had fresh, squishy, homemade honey oatmeal bread rising or baking at home. Just the smell of yeasty, fluffy bread brings me back to my mom's kitchen, where I watched her knead that dough back and forth until it was just right and ready to rest and rise on the counter.

When I became a mom, it felt natural to set aside time to make homemade honey oatmeal bread just like my mom, especially on chilly fall and winter days in New England. Something about breadmaking is relaxing physically and emotionally. I'm able to get my hands right into it and create something from a few simple ingredients. In the end, the bread feeds my body, and the kneading process nourishes my soul with its back and forth motion that provides time to think and reflect.

When I'm planning to make bread, I set aside the time, prepare the oven by preheating, get out all the tools—ingredients like flour, yeast, eggs, and water, then the bowl, mixer, and spatula.

I mix, knead, and wait.

The rising takes time.

Then I bake the bread, and the entire house smells so yummy. The aroma penetrates every room. The reward for the time and effort is sweet, chewy, homemade bread that nourishes my body and renews me.

In many ways, this time of breadmaking reminds me of the time I spend with Jesus in his Word. First, I set aside the time for him, just like I set aside time to make bread. Then I ready my heart with worship or quiet, just like I preheat the oven. Next, I get out my tools—Bible, journal, sketch pad, or music, just like I get out my bowl, mixer, and ingredients.

Finally, I wait on God to speak to me as I read, write, draw, pray, and listen to worship, just like I mix, knead, and wait for the rising of the bread.

To meet with the Lord and get to know him or to make and bake bread . . . it takes time. Time for the process. Time for the yeast to work its way through the entire ball of dough. And time for the rising, which changes the dough from simple ingredients to risen bread ready for baking. After baking, it now has a firm outer crust that protects the moist, chewy, and soft inside and keeps it fresh.

I need this time with Jesus to get to know him, to learn from him, and to sit with him like I do with a friend. Time for his Word to work its way into my soul and for it to penetrate and change me to be more like Jesus. Then when the tough stuff of life happens—and I know it will—I'll be ready because I've spent time with Jesus and his Word. I've learned how to respond to hard times with grace, humility, and love that reflect my soft heart while my outside "crust" displays my strength in him. He said, "I am the bread of life" (John 6:35) because he knows we need to get nourishment from him for our souls.

The next time the aroma of homemade bread penetrates your senses, think of Jesus, our Bread of Life, and enjoy some time in the Word being nourished by him. Then, being filled with him, you can be the aroma of Jesus wherever you go! His Word says, "for we are to God the pleasing aroma of Christ among those who are being saved and those who are perishing" (2 Cor. 2:15). This is my prayer for myself and for you as we step out into the world each day.

HONEY OATMEAL BREAD

Recipe from Linda Borio.

Yields 2 loaves

1 cup boiling water	1 cup sour cream
1½ cups rolled oats	2 eggs
⅓ cup honey	6–6½ cups unbleached flour, divided
¼ cup butter	4½ tsp dry yeast (2 packets)
1 Tbs salt	½ cup lukewarm water

1. In a large bowl, combine boiling water, oats, honey, butter, and salt. Beat together well.

2. Add sour cream, eggs, and 1½ cups of flour. Beat together well.

3. Stir in yeast (1 packet or tsp at a time) then add lukewarm water and remaining flour.

4. Dump dough out of the bowl onto a floured surface. Have extra flour ready for your hands (if needed).

5. Knead dough until it springs back when softly pushed with three fingers. This may take 5–10 minutes depending on your humidity. Use more flour on your surface and hands if dough gets sticky.

6. Cover with a clean towel, and let rise for 20 minutes. Dough will rise and may double, depending on humidity and temperature.

7. Grease two loaf pans. Divide dough in half. Gently knead each half; don't push out all the rising air. Fold over into a log to fit in your loaf pan. Cover dough with a clean towel and let rise to above the top of the loaf pans or until it is fluffy again. If you don't want to bake immediately after this second rise, you may place in refrigerator for up to 6 hours.

8. Preheat oven to 375°. Bake for 35–40 minutes, until top is light brown. Ovens may vary, so start checking bread after 35 minutes. (If baking straight from the refrigerator, let loaves stand for at least 10 minutes on the counter to get to room temp before baking.)

9. The loaves will fall from the bread pans when done and can be cooled on a wire rack (to avoid moisture making the bottom soggy). Consume while warm or toasted. Best with fresh butter, a sprinkling of cinnamon and sugar, or your favorite apple butter. The bread is moist, chewy, and soft.

Made with Love

ESSIE FAYE TAYLOR

. . . .

Better a small serving of vegetables with love than a fattened calf with hatred.
Proverbs 15:17

As a child, I often ran through my grandparents' house, laughing and content. It was the best place to be. I could have anything at Grandma and Granddad's house. There was always food, family, and faith. And the food was made with love. Grandma always had a baked cake ready to be sliced and devoured by us grandchildren. Granddad always had a surprise jar of homemade pickles. I loved a homemade pickle! I cherish those memories today, many decades later, because my grandparents are now ancestors. I remember the love with which we shared our meals and space.

Love is transformative. It's deeper than a warm fuzzy feeling or butterflies in your stomach. Love is a choice, day after day, to accept someone; it's a decision to choose that person despite their flaws, shortcomings, and idiosyncrasies. Love is patient, kind, not rude, and enduring. Love conquers all. It believes all things and hopes all things. It tolerates or bears tough things and extends grace (1 Cor. 13:4–7).

Love acts undeniably. Look at God's example. He loved humanity so much that he gave. He gave his only; he gave his all. He gave his Son so we would not perish but have everlasting life. What an incredible sacrifice.

In this text, the author declares that having a little sustenance with love is more desirable than having much sustenance with hatred. Love enhances everything in its path. Love is so transformative that it alters the atmosphere. Love often brings its brothers and sisters: peace, joy, hope, and kindness;

whereas hatred often escorts anger, fear, anxiety, jealousy, chaos, and strife. No dish would make that meal desirable. The message of the text is clear: food made with love transforms a life by feeding the soul, while hatred causes harm to the soul. Choose love.

Call to action:

1. Choose love each day. It will not be easy, but know that it will be worth it.
2. Practice walking in the transformative power of love each day. Love yourself, love God, and love others.
3. Let all that you do be governed by love, for love is the principal thing. If we speak with the tongues of angels but have no love, our actions are purposeless (1 Cor. 13:1). Food absent of love is unfulfilling and empty.
4. Know that because of love, our lives have been transformed. We have been renewed and given life abundant and eternal. Extend love to others so that they might see your love and be drawn to the true lover of our souls.
5. Remember, love wins. Even when hatred rears its ugly head in situations, love conquers all. God is love.

Ordinary Abundance

COURTNEY ZONNEFELD

· · · ·

Speak to them, saying, "At twilight you shall eat meat, and in the morning you shall be filled with bread. And you shall know that I am the LORD your God."

Exodus 16:12 NKJV

When the workday ends, I long to be in the kitchen. I pull on my apron and exhale. My first goal is dinner, probably something that makes enough for tomorrow's lunch. But sometimes I make a simple dinner so I can focus my energies on something more unnecessary. I clear my counters in order to dirty them again. I find a cookbook or scroll through my phone for a recipe, turn on a playlist or my current favorite album, and begin to bake.

During the day I work with my head; at night I want to work with my hands. I crave the creativity and stability of baking. I love the way a recipe unfolds like a carefully choreographed dance: planned yet somehow new every time the steps start again. Maybe the day—the week—has been long, hard, and stressful. Maybe it has been joyful or rewarding. But all that disappears into the rhythms of the recipe. I can't concentrate on my own schedule. I have to focus on zesting a lime, rotating a mixing bowl, scraping its sides with a spatula. I need to shape dough into a ball, roll it out, cut it into shapes, slide baking sheets into the oven, and wait.

In Genesis, after six days of creating, God rests. His work has not been cruel, tiring, or oppressive. He simply declares that it is time to rest. On Mount Sinai, he declares rest yet again: this time, as a regular habit for his people. Perhaps—even after seeing God split the Red Sea in two—his people need the reminder that they are not the most powerful force in their world.

Even when the Israelites grumble, God provides them with bread and meat from heaven. Still, they must not gather this food on Sabbath, the day of rest and remembering.

When I bake, I remember that I am more than work, even if the workday was a good one. As I create, I become grounded in my own body, in my own place in creation. I am not the creator of everything that is good. Some good things I just get to participate in, like measuring out baking powder so the cake batter rises into a perfect dome. I can sit back and watch while something amazing happens behind the oven door.

Time in the kitchen settles my soul. As I read recipes and combine ingredients, I find a moment of Sabbath, of God's presence breaking through my routines and somehow transforming them. Returning to the kitchen can be a way to cling to joy, even when I am exhausted.

By the time my baked goods are cooling on their racks, I know where I will deliver them. Many nights cookies only travel to a container left on my dining table, where my housemate and I periodically open the lid and slip out a snack or after-dinner treat. Other times, I pack up a cake or bars for family, friends, or an event. Or I stack up containers of shortbread for coworkers, neighbors, or a tired friend. Whenever a recipe makes more than enough, I know that these baked goods can't just sit on my countertop and spoil. They are meant to be shared.

On Sundays, Saturdays, and holidays, I often bake something elaborate and complicated—something special, a feast that ripples through the week. But the food we cook and bake on ordinary days might be even more important. When we make something with our hands on Mondays, workdays, or dreary days, we insist that life can be full of joy, even when its events are not. We shout out that abundance can look like scarcity, that God's provision is not restricted to the days we call good.

GINGER-LIME SHORTBREAD COOKIES

Yields 3 dozen

For the shortbread

1 cup unsalted butter (2 sticks), softened

zest of 2 small limes

1 tsp ground ginger

½ cup powdered sugar

2 cups all-purpose flour

½ tsp salt

For decoration

white or clear sprinkles (or coarse sparkling sugar) *Or*

¼ cup dark chocolate chips + 1–2 tsp coconut oil or vegetable shortening

(or dark chocolate melting wafers) and flaky sea salt

1. Place softened butter in a large bowl. Zest limes into butter and add ground ginger. Use a flexible spatula to smash and blend the butter with the zest and ginger. Set aside for at least an hour and a half—the longer you let the lime and ginger "steep" into the butter, the stronger the flavors will be.

2. Preheat oven to 350° and grease two baking sheets. Set aside.

3. Cream butter to a fluffy consistency. Add powdered sugar, flour, and salt, then mix with your spatula until a soft and crumbly dough starts to form. If you were short on time for steeping the butter, taste the dough at this step and test whether you might want stronger flavor. Add additional lime zest or ginger ¼ tsp at a time, if desired. Then finish forming the dough; I usually switch to using my hands to press the dough together and avoid overworking it. (Overworked dough will not produce a flaky cookie.)

4. Roll dough onto a lightly floured surface until about ¼ inch thick. Cut out cookies with your cutter of choice—something seasonal, or perhaps an upside-down Mason jar. Place on prepared cookie sheet. If decorating with sugar or sprinkles, lightly sprinkle them over the shortbread at this point.

5. Bake for 12–14 minutes. If the cookies feel dry to the touch and do not break apart when you try to lift them with a spatula, then they're ready to come out of the oven. Leave on the baking sheet for 2 minutes to set up, then remove to a wire rack or parchment paper to cool.

6. If decorating with chocolate, set cooled shortbread on a sheet of parchment paper. Place dark chocolate and shortening or coconut oil in a small bowl and microwave on high in 30-second intervals, stirring in between, until the chocolate drips easily off a fork. (If using wafers, melt according to package directions.)

7. If the chocolate does not drip easily, thin the mixture by adding a little more shortening or coconut oil, ½ tsp at a time, and heating for 15-second intervals.

8. Use a fork to flick the melted chocolate across the cookies, creating long, thin, and sometimes intersecting lines of chocolate. Continue until you're satisfied with the look; I find I usually need to stop earlier than I expect. Sprinkle a small amount of flaky sea salt on top of the chocolate before it hardens. Let cool. Store in an airtight container. Shortbread will freeze well for about 2–3 months.

Resurrecting Bananas

LESLIE M. BOSSERMAN

· · · ·

For since we believe that Jesus died and rose again, even so, through Jesus, God will bring with him those who have fallen asleep. . . . Therefore encourage one another with these words.

1 Thessalonians 4:14, 18 ESV

"Mom, look!" my five-year-old shared with excitement, holding up an overripe banana. "It's a cheetah!"

Smiling with curiosity, I noticed brown spots had formed just like cheetah print along both sides of the banana. I picked up the rest of the bunch and declared, "Wow! We have a whole *coalition* of cheetahs invading our kitchen." (After watching too many episodes of *Wild Kratts*, my now-educated Mom Brain knows that packs of cheetahs are called coalitions.)

"There's only one thing to do," I said, pausing for dramatic effect as my seven-year-old son joined the kitchen party, along with his two-year-old little sister. "It's time to turn this bunch of cheetah bananas into something tasty!"

A chorus of excited cheers erupted from my three kids as we brought down our beloved red KitchenAid mixer and donned aprons. We own a local preschool, which means we seem to bring home bunches of overripe bananas at the end of each week—which means we get creative in the kitchen!

Now it seems like, most Sundays, we have gotten into the practice of "resurrecting" bananas: taking something that might have been discarded or thought to be too ripe and turning it into something tasty and universally enjoyable. What once started as a fun baking experiment has become a healthy routine around our kitchen island.

Is your relationship with Jesus like these cheetah bananas?

During your busy week, do you forget about him until you notice that spots have formed, and he calls you back into the kitchen to become a new creation?

In fact, that's exactly Jesus's business: taking something that might have been discarded or deemed past its prime and redeeming it or even resurrecting it.

Meeting Martha at her brother Lazarus's tomb after he died, Jesus said to her, "I am the resurrection and the life. Whoever believes in me, though he die, yet shall he live, and everyone who lives and believes in me shall never die. Do you believe this?" (John 11:25–26 ESV).

Do *you* believe this?

Just as Jesus lived a perfect life and died on the cross to cover all our sins, he has also been resurrected into eternal life and will return at the sound of a fanfare of trumpets, and we will be with our Lord again—for eternity (1 Thess. 4:13–18; Rev. 11:15).

Let this powerful truth and promise sink in. We will not stay as spotted cheetah bananas. We, too, shall be changed in the twinkling of an eye.

> Just as we have borne the image of the man of dust, we shall also bear the image of the man of heaven. I tell you this, brothers: flesh and blood cannot inherit the kingdom of God, nor does the perishable inherit the imperishable. Behold! I tell you a mystery. We shall not all sleep, but we shall all be changed, in a moment, in the twinkling of an eye, at the last trumpet. For the trumpet will sound, and the dead will be raised imperishable, and we shall be changed. (1 Cor. 15:49–52 ESV)

And until Jesus returns, we have important work to do. Inner work to both heal and reveal who he intends us to become. Outer work to show up and serve our families, communities, and churches who need to hear this message of redemption and revival. And it starts by noticing our own spots and choosing to do something about them.

"CHEETAH" BANANA BREAD

Yields 1 loaf

½ cup butter (1 stick), softened
1 cup sugar
2 eggs, beaten
3 overripe "cheetah" bananas, peeled and finely mashed (for extra moist and delicious banana bread, try 4 bananas)

1½ cups flour
1 tsp baking soda
½ tsp salt

Optional add-ins

½ tsp vanilla
1 tsp cinnamon
1 tsp nutmeg

¼ cup chopped walnuts
¼ cup shredded coconut
½ cup chocolate chips

1. Preheat oven to 350°.

2. Beat together butter and sugar.

3. Add eggs and mashed bananas.

4. Combine well.

5. Sift together flour, soda, and salt. Add to creamed mixture.

6. Stir in any additional ingredients as desired. Mix just until combined. Do not overmix.

7. Pour into greased and floured loaf pan.

8. Bake at 350° for 55 minutes (check at 45 minutes, depending on your oven), until golden brown.

9. Keeps well for 5–7 days, refrigerated.

Simmer Down

TYRA LANE-KINGSLAND

. . . .

For God has not given us a spirit of fear, but of power and of love and of a sound mind.
2 Timothy 1:7 NKJV

You're wearing your shoulders for earrings," came the gentle reminder from my friend, a trauma-informed psychologist. And she was right. Whenever I get fearful, stressed, or anxious, my whole body gets rigid, and I draw my shoulders up toward my ears.

Have you ever been there? Has the enemy's chatter caused you to cower in fear? Has a tremendous load of worry and doubt left you buckling under its weight? While it's happened to me more times than I'd like to admit, I have found a space that serves as a refuge from the noise and a sanctuary from the storms. I get to visit this special place daily. This place is a war room, prayer room, and communal room all in one. It's a place that doesn't require fancy decor. This place is my kitchen.

The kitchen isn't merely a place for preparing food; it's a place of encountering. Just as Martha had an encounter with Jesus amid her kitchen duties, we, too, can experience changes in our perspective as we go about preparing our meals. Your kitchen is a food prep center and prayer closet all wrapped in one. Your counter provides the perfect leverage for elbows to rest upon in prayer and your sink the container for bottling your tears (Ps. 56:8).

In today's verse, the apostle Paul gives us a recipe on how to win the internal battle that can rage in our hearts and minds. And right here in our kitchens, we can secure the victory. In the kitchen, we are warring on our own turf. In the kitchen, we've got the home-court advantage. In a world that's chaotic, there is stability in sliding out our cutting board, and there is a gentle reassurance in the orderliness of our spice rack. As meal preparation commences, so does donning our spiritual armor. Ingredients are our arsenal; salt is a sword and spinach a shield. Negative thoughts are lacerated and brought into the obedience of Christ. In the symphony of preparing a meal, we tame fear and open the door to power, love, and a sound mind.

Some translations of this verse use the words *timidity* or *cowardice* in place of *fear*. When we set out to cook, we don't approach the ingredients with timidity. With boldness, we slice through onions even if they produce tears. With precision, we dice carrots and celery, and in the rhythmic motions we unwind from the stressors of the day. With focused attention, we pour our hearts into our cooking, imbuing our dishes with love. The mere act of cooking slows us down and brings us fully into the present. In a world that is unpredictable, there is a surety and peace to be garnered from time spent in the kitchen.

To this day, I can vividly recall the words on the vintage trivet that hung in my grandmother's kitchen: "No matter where I serve my guests it seems they like my kitchen best." Your kitchen is the hub where bellies are filled and where souls can simmer down. May your kitchen continue to be a conduit of power, love, and a sound mind for all who enter it.

APPLE BAKED OATMEAL

Serves 8

1 Tbs ground flax
3 Tbs water
2 cups old-fashioned rolled oats
⅓ cup chopped walnuts
2 tsp baking powder
¼ tsp salt
1 tsp cinnamon

½ cup coconut sugar
2 cups almond milk
⅓ cup coconut oil
2 tsp pure vanilla extract
2 baking apples (like Granny Smith),
    peeled, cored, and diced

1. Preheat oven to 350°.

2. Place flax and water in a small bowl and whisk vigorously, then set aside to rest at least 5 minutes.

3. In a large bowl, combine oats, nuts, baking powder, salt, and cinnamon.

4. In another bowl, whisk together sugar, milk, oil, vanilla, and flax egg. Stir wet mixture into oat mixture.

5. Place apples into a greased 9×13 baking pan, then pour oat mixture over. Bake for 40 minutes, or until set and golden on top.

The Hidden Ingredient

ANDREA DOERING

· · · ·

Let me teach you; for I am gentle and humble, and you shall find rest for your souls;
for I give you only light burdens.

Matthew 11:29–30 TLB

Our family loves to have pita and hummus as a snack or a light meal, and when our three children were living at home, we needed a lot of pita! So I started making it myself, as a cost-saving measure. But that's not the reason I keep making it, now that we're empty nesters. Now it's because of a lesson I relearn each week as I pull out the simple ingredients.

If you were to look on my kitchen counter, you would see yeast, flour, water, salt, and shortening. But there's an ingredient missing, the one that grounds me into a spiritual practice each week: time to rest.

My recipe calls for several short rest periods for the dough, just ten minutes each. The dough takes that time for the gluten to relax. As one recipe says, "It gives it a chance to loosen and unwind." Now that's a good idea for humans too! So while my dough rests, I do too. I read a few pages of a book. I look out the kitchen window at the trees. I listen to music. I make a cup of tea. Mostly, I just enjoy ten minutes of rest. Then there's a short next step, and then another rest. By the time the dough and I have finished our work, we have rested together for forty minutes.

All this requires of me is the patience to wait. Because I could choose to ignore the rest. I could bang that dough into pita shapes and bake it right away. I'd have something that looked like pita, and it wouldn't take as long. But I would miss so much. I would miss the magic of what happens when yeast mixes with flour and is given time. I would miss what happens to me when I trust a process rather than pushing my own schedule, which is not based on knowledge of the process. I would miss truly being aware of my present moment. And I'm pretty sure my family would miss the taste of the final product they've come to expect.

So many times, God's people are told to rest. We are informed that God himself rested in the act of creation. And it's interesting that in Exodus 31:17, God tells Moses to say to the Israelites that the Sabbath "is a sign forever between me and the people of Israel that in six days the LORD made heaven and earth, and on the seventh day he rested and was refreshed" (ESV). In *Sabbath*, Wayne Muller writes that "the [Hebrew] word 'refreshed,' *vaiynafesh*, literally means, 'and God exhaled.'"* He suggests that after six days of the inhale—creation—the resting period of the seventh day is the exhale, and that "without the Sabbath exhale, the life-giving inhale is impossible."** It makes me think that creation—of the world, or of anything—is not complete without rest.

For me, making pita each week, letting the dough and myself rest and relax as we go, is a way to embody the trust relationship between myself and God.

---

* Wayne Muller, *Sabbath: Finding Rest, Renewal, and Delight in Our Busy Lives* (New York: Bantam, 1999), 36.
** Muller, *Sabbath*, 36.

Savoring God's Goodness

APRIL JOHNSON

· · · ·

Taste and see that the LORD is good. Oh, the joys of those who take refuge in him!
Psalm 34:8 NLT

When I am feeling low or experiencing life's challenges, I find solace in dining out with a trusted friend. By the end of the evening, I feel uplifted and have had a good laugh. It is my happy place, a surefire way to boost my mood no matter the obstacles I face. Whether it's financial struggles, unruly kids, work issues, or a troubled marriage, the gift of laughter from a good friend is powerful medicine.

My friend and I enjoy dining at great restaurants where we can indulge in delicious food and engaging conversation. Her amusing and witty personality never fails to make me laugh, whether it's through her words or facial expressions. It's remarkable how, even after a satisfying meal, we still manage to laugh so much. If we go for months without seeing each other, we always make plans to get together for dinner. Meeting up and looking forward to trying new dishes is always a delightful experience.

Psalm 34 portrays God's kindness to us through two of our most valuable senses: taste and sight. Think about when you've savored a flawlessly cooked dish. When my friend and I have done so on some occasions, our delight is evident to those around us. The savory and succulent taste is unforgettable. The dish's presentation is visually appealing enough to entice others at a nearby table to order the same meal or even return to the restaurant for it.

As much as I enjoy being with my good friend and having good food, it will never compare to tasting and seeing the goodness of God. His faithfulness alone is praiseworthy. To experience the feeling of God's goodness and love is indescribable. To know God loves us enough to send his only Son to die for us demonstrates the depth of his love and how he continues to offer us the opportunity to taste and see his love.

Tasting and seeing God's *agape* love brings immense joy through intimate communion with him. This is a powerful and gracious encounter.

Through God's love, we are saved, healed, renewed, and revitalized. He always provides us an opportunity to repent and return to his love and mercy. We can experience and witness God's presence in our lives.

God's very existence can be seen and tasted. And it is indeed good.

RED VELVET GOOEY BUTTER CAKE

Serves 15

1 red velvet cake mix
3 eggs, divided
1 cup butter (2 sticks), softened and divided

8 oz cream cheese, softened
1 tsp vanilla extract
1 lb powdered sugar, divided

1. Preheat oven to 350°. Grease a 9×13 pan.

2. In a large bowl, mix cake mix, 1 egg, and 1 stick butter until thoroughly combined.

3. Pour mixture into pan and spread evenly.

4. In a separate bowl, mix cream cheese, vanilla, remaining eggs, and remaining butter until smooth.

5. Set aside ¼ cup powdered sugar, then add remaining sugar to the cream cheese mix and blend until smooth.

6. Pour cream cheese mixture over cake batter and spread evenly.

7. Bake for 40–50 minutes, or until the center is firmly set.

8. After removing the cake from the oven, sprinkle with reserved powdered sugar while it's still warm.

Simmer in His Presence

KARYNTHIA GLASPER PHILLIPS

· · · ·

Be not hasty to go out of his sight.
Ecclesiastes 8:3 KJV

Cooking is an exciting fine art requiring lots of attention. However, as a child, I always wanted to complete my assigned task for the meal as quickly as possible and dash out the door to play. My mom would begin cooking our dinner meal in the morning after my four sisters and I went to school. On the days one of us stayed home from school, we would find ourselves in the kitchen assisting Momma with cooking.

Out of school at home, feeling better as I recovered from a cold, I learned to make soup—Momma's seasoned stewed chicken. Like a baby hawk, I watched the pot until it began to boil with all the ingredients that seemed to rise to the top. Then we turned the eye of the stove down while inhaling the flavorful aroma. In Momma's kitchen, as the skimmer, I was taught early on to move slowly, handle the fat-rich broth carefully, and not throw any of the fat away.

Momma would remind me of the enriched broth's usefulness for cooking other things, like soups, dumplings, and gravy, or thinning a pot of thick soup. She would say, "The enriched broth is where the flavor and nutrients for the meal are."

Recently, while preparing kale soup, I thought about my "skimming" off the top of God's Word and throwing the fat away. In my personal prayer time, I began to notice I was hurrying through my Bible reading, writing, and reflection. I observed my haste. I was throwing away spiritual nutrients by not giving myself time to draw spiritual insights. Instead, I was quick to put down my Bible and journal and pick up my daily planner.

Standing and stirring my soup at the stove, I sensed the presence of God calm my thoughts as I watched the ingredients swirl around in the pot. The stillness intensified as I transferred some of the rich broth to a bowl. I began humming a worship song and meditating on Scripture. The slow stillness turned into a time of blessing for me. Doing life at a fast pace can put us in a whirlwind that distracts us. Often, we struggle to find ourselves, or we're unclear about how to pursue goals and dreams. When we limit our time with God, we limit our capacity to receive from his life-giving presence.

How many times have you hurriedly read a passage of Scripture, quickly jotted down a few thoughts, and later couldn't recall the verse or the relevant message, if any, discerned during your devotional time? Suppose you are moving through life at breakneck speed with a planner filled with appointments and no significant time designated for quality time with God or for savoring the atmosphere of God's presence as you meditate on the Word—like me. In that case, you might be "tossing the fat."

Slow reading, writing, and reflection equip us to savor all that God brings to the surface of our hearts. In meditation, we find that time in God's presence is "profitable for doctrine, for reproof, for correction, for instruction in righteousness" (2 Tim. 3:16 KJV). As our taste for God grows, our desire to dig deeper into the Word grows too. I have learned to move slowly to let the richness of God's Word rise to the top, gathering revelation and strategies for my day. The Spirit of Truth enables Scripture to rise in our hearts, teaching the value of the Word of God. It is a recipe for daily victorious Christian living.

Let your time with God stir slowly. Slow down to prevent skimming off the top of the Word; it contains relevant nutrients for spiritual maturity. Let's continue to glean wisdom, knowledge, and strength for life in God's presence.

KALE SOUP

Serves 6–8

1 Tbs extra-virgin olive oil
2 cups low-sodium chicken broth
2 cups water
1 bag chopped kale (or 1 lg bunch, stems removed and chopped)
1 clove garlic, minced
½ tsp crushed red pepper
½ tsp sea salt
½ tsp freshly ground black pepper (optional)

½ yellow onion, finely chopped, divided
2 (15.5 oz) cans cannellini beans, drained and rinsed (optional)
1–2 precooked boneless skinless chicken breasts, chopped (optional)
1–2 lg sweet potatoes, diced
freshly grated Parmesan or feta cheese for serving

1. In a large pot over medium heat, add olive oil, broth, and water. Bring to a simmer. Slowly add kale, allowing it to cook down before adding more. Once all the kale is in the pot, add garlic, crushed red pepper, salt, and pepper, if using. Add half of the onion, then cook until slightly soft and fragrant.

2. If using, add the beans and cooked chicken. Turn heat down to low and simmer. Add additional broth ½ cup at a time if soup is too thick.

3. Continue to simmer for 30 minutes. Add the remaining onion. When the kale leaves are smooth and wilted, the kale is done. Add diced sweet potatoes and cook until softened to your liking.

4. Garnish per your preference with Parmesan or feta cheese before serving.

The Ingredients of God's Character

ROBIN BUPP

· · · ·

The LORD is good, a stronghold in the day of trouble; he knows those who take refuge in him.

Nahum 1:7 ESV

A tasty hot beverage is a necessary component of my time in the Word. As I was making a mug of hot chocolate the other day, I licked some stray cocoa off my finger; I was promptly reminded that though these ingredients are delicious in combination, cocoa alone is bitter. In fact, although I'd be willing to eat the other ingredients of hot chocolate on their own, it is the depth and complexity of their commingling that makes the drink so pleasing.

I love it when my Bible reading plan lands me in a passage about God's love or a story that highlights his provision. Being reminded of his nearness or his wisdom sets me off into the day with a hopeful heart and a positive outlook. There are many stories of the characteristics of God that easily make us feel peace, hope, joy, and comfort. But sometimes a Bible reading plan can land you in a spot like the book of Nahum.

The first six verses of Nahum are rather striking. Here's a quick sampling: "the LORD takes vengeance and is filled with wrath" (v. 2), "the LORD will not leave the guilty unpunished" (v. 3), and "Who can endure his fierce anger? His wrath is poured out like fire; the rocks are shattered before him" (v. 6). Not the morning pick-me-up I was hoping for (at least not at first glance!), and just about as jarring as eating a big spoonful of plain cocoa powder.

In my particular printing of the Bible, these verses claim nearly the entire first column of the page. One lone verse is set apart below: "The LORD is good, a refuge in times of trouble" (v. 7). Nahum is sharing about God's jealous anger and his vengeance. Then he is inspired to write, "the LORD is good." All of the anger, vengeance, and punishment discussed in these verses can be trusted in God's hands because he is good. The Hebrew for the word translated "good" here means a lot of the things you would think it would mean—pleasant, acceptable, excellent—but it also means *ethically right*. He's completely good in every sense of the word.

God's wrath can be hard to swallow. Without sugar (and milk), cocoa is hard to swallow, but I know that it is good! It might be bitter alone, but that's why I don't eat it alone. God's wrath is never the only part of his character; he is always all of who he is, all the time. If I did not trust God's goodness or know of his mercy and grace to me through Jesus Christ, his wrath would be hard to swallow. It's the totality of God's character that makes him worthy of our right reverence and awe.

Cocoa, and this passage in Nahum, remind me that I can trust God—when I don't understand, when I don't have any idea what he's working out—because he is good. The fullness of his character, all together and not in parts, is worthy of my praise and my delight.

Someone's in the Kitchen with Martha

KATIE M. REID

. . . .

The Lord replied, "My Presence will go with you, and I will give you rest."
Exodus 33:14

Martha scurries to and fro, trying to get everything just right for her honored guests. Jesus and his disciples have come to visit, and there are many last-minute tasks to complete, but her sister, Mary, sits at Jesus's feet instead of helping her. Martha takes her complaint and frustration to Jesus, asking him to tell Mary to "help a sister out!"

I have always been a fan of biblical Martha because I relate to her: a get-it-done gal who feels ultra-responsible and just wants to do the right thing but sometimes feels alone in her quest of bringing order to the mess.

In the account of Martha and Mary found in Luke 10:38–42, we read that Jesus does not intervene in the way Martha expects. Rather he corrects Martha, telling her she is worried and distracted about many things, and commends Mary for choosing the better thing (vv. 41–42).

Jesus's response used to irritate me. I longed for the story to go differently, yet the more I studied this passage, the more my angst melted away like butter in a fry pan as I saw something I had missed.

First of all, I had confused Jesus's correction with rejection. He loves Martha (John 11:5), and because he does, he treats her like a daughter by correcting her. We read throughout Scripture that Jesus disciplines those he loves (see Heb. 12:6). If my child is off course, it is loving to point it out with gentleness, firmness, and respect, so they have an opportunity to course correct before they go too far down a road that might lead to destruction.

Unless Jesus and his disciples are fasting while they are at Martha's home, or he's going to multiply loaves and fish again, someone has to prepare the meal for them. So I'm not sure Jesus is asking Martha to sit down physically in that moment, but I think he is inviting her to sit down from a spiritual standpoint. He's reminding her who is in her home: her friend, Jesus. Her soul can be at rest even while her hands are busy because he is with her: Immanuel, "God with us."

Whether you are scurrying around prepping a meal for guests, carting kids around to their activities, or rushing to complete a work deadline, Jesus is with you in it all. Yes, sitting at his feet is a good and necessary thing, but a relationship with Jesus that feeds your soul, like the hearty beef stew my family adores, is one where you are aware of his sustaining presence throughout your day and enjoy his company.

Even though Jesus may have been in the other room teaching his disciples, he's there with Martha in the kitchen too, ever-present, offering a healthy portion of peace to his dear friend. Martha's gift of service to her guests isn't the problem; the issue is that she's serving from a place of angst and frustration—seeing the lack instead of focusing on the lavish gift of Jesus in her midst.

Jesus's presence, the Holy Spirit, is with you, even in those angsty, frustrating moments. He can help you shift your focus from what seems amiss to the blessings all around you he doesn't want you to miss! His peace that passes all understanding never runs out—there is enough of him to go around and fill you up to overflowing.

MARTHA'S HEARTY BEEF STEW

Serves 4–6

1–2 lbs venison tenderloin
  or beef chuck
2 cups beef broth
1 packet Italian dressing seasoning
1 packet onion soup mix
1 packet beef gravy seasoning

5 carrots, peeled and chopped
5 med yellow or red potatoes, diced to
  the size you prefer, peeled or not
1 tsp thyme
sea salt to taste
fresh-cracked black pepper to taste

1. Chop meat and season with salt and pepper, then add to a slow cooker with remaining ingredients. Stir to thoroughly combine.

2. Cook for 6 hours on low, stirring again partway through. Serve on top of rice or noodles if desired.

Good Eatin'

ESSIE FAYE TAYLOR

. . . .

If you are willing and obedient, you will eat the good things of the land.
Isaiah 1:19

As I stared into the heavens, I felt defeated. Honestly, I was depressed; I was in a very dark valley of my life. I had been faithful to God and served him with all my heart. I married a believer; I kept myself pure until I married. I practiced holiness. Yet my life fell apart; my heart was shattered when my marriage ended in divorce. "How could this happen, Lord?!" I screamed from within. The pain and grief I experienced were heavy. It was as if there was a dark cloud hovering over me that I couldn't seem to shake.

As believers, we are not excluded from life's trials. We experience loss, pain, disease, heartbreak, betrayal, and so on. Although our faith does not make us exempt, our faith does sustain us in these trying times. During difficulty, we must believe the text above: if we obey God, we will experience the best of life—we will *eat good*. We will be full and satisfied naturally and spiritually. God will see to it. In essence, it is believing that something good is coming from the pain we are experiencing. The eagle-eyed prophet Isaiah declares God's truth. God walked closely with him through tough times and victorious times. He saw the Lord high and lifted up, and he saw God perform miracles in discouraging situations. He affirms God's faithfulness.

The apostle Paul also declares God's faithfulness, saying, "And we know that in all things God works for the good of those who love him, who have been called according to his purpose" (Rom. 8:28). Paul states that we are certain of this thing—sometimes we need to remind ourselves of this truth.

We must hold fast to it in the midst of life's storms. Many times our circumstances seem to disprove the truth of God, but "in all things God works for the good" means that something good is coming from this bad situation. God's going to turn it around.

The patriarch and wise man Joseph declared that what the devil meant for evil in his life, God used for good. Joseph was betrayed, sold into slavery, lied about, and thrown into prison for years, but God had a plan to save his people by Joseph's hand. We've got to believe God is faithful and his Word is true. If we are obedient, we will consume everything good. The fat of the land represents prosperity in mind, body, and soul. Although now we are dissatisfied, disappointed, and depressed, if we faithfully obey God, we will be satisfied and full. Good eatin' always brings joy and dancing. That is our portion.

Call to action:

1. Hold fast to the promises of God in the midst of your life's storms. He is faithful and will keep every promise.
2. Believe that something good will come from your bad experience. Reframe your experience. You are not a victim; you are a victor.
3. Be obedient to God's commands and statutes. In doing so, you will make your way prosperous.
4. Lean in to your relationship with God during difficult times. Find comfort in the secret place of prayer. Lean in to your relationships with loved ones. Love heals and comforts.
5. Remember, God has good thoughts toward you and good plans for your life, "plans to give you hope and a future" (Jer. 29:11).

The Miracle of Marinating

JILL NOBLE

· · · ·

Remain in me, as I also remain in you. No branch can bear fruit by itself; it must remain in the vine. Neither can you bear fruit unless you remain in me.

John 15:4

Before we were engaged, my now-husband asked if I liked to cook. Casually I answered with, "No, not really." But I didn't want to admit I didn't know how to cook anything, so I added quickly, "But I like to bake!" hoping that would impress him.

I grew up in a home where I was shoo-shooed from the kitchen. I learned on my own to make brownies from a box and cookies from a refrigerated tube of dough. A frozen pizza was nearing the limit of my culinary expertise, and the extent of my knowledge of spices was limited to salt and pepper, though I wonder if I ever used them. As a single woman, I mostly lived on breakfast cereal.

When we married, I was as young and inexperienced in my faith journey as I was in the kitchen. I learned to read my Bible and walk with Jesus while educating myself on many other things, like how to read a cookbook and prepare food.

Most of the Bible was new to me. It was only a few years earlier that I'd discovered there was an Old Testament that went along with and came before the New Testament! In the Lord's kindness, he gave me a teachable heart and an insatiable appetite for learning. This hunger served me well when I bent over my Bible as well as when I was apron-clad and finding my way in the kitchen.

In those days, I noticed something as I listened to others talk about reading their Bibles. Some people seemed to use the Bible like they would use spices from their kitchens to liven up their food—a little soy sauce here, some salt and pepper there. They were applying those Bible verses commonly printed on T-shirts and mugs about sadness, perseverance, or joy, but never opening—really opening—and lingering in their Bibles, dwelling with God. Dabbling briefly and haphazardly in the Word of God is similar to adding spices to the outside of meat: it only touches the outside and does not permeate the middle.

In my early years of faith and homemaking, I learned to apply a wonder-producing word in both arenas: *marinate*.

To marinate is to undergo a soaking. Soaking up the Word of God and dwelling in it for extended periods is like plopping a pork chop into a marinade and leaving it there for a while. Marinating in God's Word changes our character, just like marinating meat revolutionizes its texture.

There is a man in our church who has memorized much of the New Testament. Occasionally, to offer encouragement and accountability, I'll ask him, "What are you soaking up now?" When he memorizes Scripture, his soul is marinating in the life-giving Word of God. He intentionally and thoughtfully dwells in a place that will change him from the inside out.

How do we marinate in the Word of God? Here are some suggestions:

1. Memorize the Word and read it out loud slowly.
2. Sing the Scriptures. Several fantastic artists have produced songs that sing word for word through Scripture passages.
3. Fellowship with others over the Word of God.
4. Journal your thoughts and reflections as you read. Get used to reading your Bible with a pen in hand.

The result of marinating in the Bible, by God's grace, will change a person from the inside out and result in a soul more yielded, a spirit more enlightened, and a heart more tender to him and others.

MARINATED PORK CHOPS

Serves 4

Marinade

⅓ cup soy sauce
2 Tbs brown sugar
2 tsp Worcestershire sauce
1 tsp Dijon mustard
2 cloves garlic, minced
½ tsp black pepper

4 bone-in pork chops (about 1 inch
    thick)
1 Tbs olive oil
salt and pepper

1. Place all marinade ingredients in a resealable plastic bag. Gently massage to combine.

2. Pat pork chops dry with paper towels, then rub with olive oil and drop them into the resealable bag. Turn the sealed bag repeatedly until pork chops are thoroughly coated in marinade.

3. Place the bag in the refrigerator for at least 3 hours, turning occasionally. Take pork chops out of the fridge and remove them from the bag 20 minutes before cooking. Set marinade aside for later.

4. Brush a barbecue grill with oil and preheat to medium-high. Remove excess marinade from pork chops and season lightly with salt and pepper as desired.

5. Place pork on preheated grill and cook for 4 minutes or until pork releases from the grill, then flip and cook for 3 more minutes.

6. Baste both sides with reserved marinade, then cook each side for 30 more seconds, which will make a delicious crust. Chops should be removed when their internal temperature is between 145° and 150°.

7. Transfer chops to a plate, cover loosely with foil, and let rest for 5 minutes before serving.

Note: thin pork chops tend to dry out more easily. Bone-in pork chops usually take a little more time to cook but tend to be juicier than boneless pork chops.

To cook in the oven: preheat oven to 425°. Line a rimmed baking sheet with parchment paper. Bake pork chops for about 20 minutes for 1-inch chops. Don't overcook! Take chops out when their internal temperature is between 145° and 150°. Let rest for 5 minutes, loosely covered with foil, before serving.

Counting the Cost

KRISTEN D. FARRELL

· · · ·

Therefore I tell you, do not worry about your life, what you will eat or drink; or about your body, what you will wear. Is not life more than food, and the body more than clothes? Look at the birds of the air; they do not sow or reap or store away in barns, and yet your heavenly Father feeds them. Are you not much more valuable than they?

Matthew 6:25–26

Most of us have a complicated relationship with food. I know I do. On one hand, I don't want extra carbs, too much sugar, or excess gluten. On the other hand, I want to indulge in the cranberry orange scones I made with my son recently. Even better, include a rich dark roast coffee topped with luxurious heavy cream left over from the recipe. But I'd be lying if I said it was an easy choice. And lately, life feels filled with a million little choices. Most are mundane and fairly inconsequential but worthy of a modicum of worry.

And there is seemingly a lot to worry about. As a mom, I've heard the mantra repeated over and over that goes something like this: "The dishes can wait. Your kids won't be young forever. Spend time with them instead." And even as I know this and have seen it to be true, I also know that waking up to a sink full of dishes with crusted cheese and smeared ketchup from last night's dinner is just, well, gross. Clean house or engaged parenting? Sometimes I feel like I spend the whole day weighing out the cost of nearly *everything*. If I watch a show with my husband tonight after bedtime, I'll pay for it at 5:30 a.m. when the alarm goes off and I wake up groggier than usual. If I toss the football after school with one of my sons, I'll miss my window for a "real" workout at the gym. If I skip my favorite soft serve twist when my family celebrates a musical well performed, will I send the message to my teenage daughter that ice cream is bad? It. Is. Exhausting.

And yet, Jesus's words from the Sermon on the Mount remind us of a simple truth: he's got us covered.

Although it is the responsibility of a fully functioning human to be thoughtful and intentional about such things, at the end of the day, he's got this. Following Jesus should be a life of following freedom. Of pursuing his truths again and again until we finally feel the love, value, acceptance, care, and generosity that only the freedom of our faith can and should bring.

"Do not worry" sounds like flippant advice. A well-meaning platitude easily contradicted by something like, "Yeah, Jesus, but if you knew my story, my struggle, my suffering, you wouldn't make it sound that easy." And you're right. It isn't easy.

In Matthew 6, Jesus doesn't try to downplay our experiences, our pain. He doesn't say food and clothes are unnecessary or futile pursuits. He does offer this: perspective and provision. What is worthy of our worry? What is worthy of our angst, indecision, and unrest?

In other words, most of our decisions aren't moral ones that question our integrity or our character. Jesus offers us perspective because he assures us of his provision. You see, these worries in our everyday physical lives can easily shift our focus away from a very significant truth: we are valuable *regardless* of our social status, socioeconomic position, or ability to attain worldly recognition. Aren't you more valuable than the birds, regardless of what your boss says, what the scale says, what your savings account says? Jesus says you are worthy of the care he will provide.

So have the scone or skip it? Either. Just don't worry about it.

SCONES FOR THE NON-BAKER

Yields 8 scones

2 cups flour
½ tsp salt
1 Tbs baking powder
2 Tbs sugar

½ cup butter (1 stick), chilled and cut
 into small chunks
½ cup dried cranberries
zest from 1 orange
¾ cup heavy cream

1. Preheat oven to 400°. Grease 8 cups of a muffin pan.

2. Whisk dry ingredients together first, then cut in butter with a pastry blender or two knives to make pebble-sized meal. Add cranberries and orange zest.

3. Mix in heavy cream so a batter forms. You may need to add a little more to absorb all dry ingredients. Dough will be thick but malleable.

4. Spoon dough into muffin pan to keep a circular shape. Drizzle a little extra heavy cream on top.

5. Bake for 12–15 minutes or until golden brown on top. Let scones sit in pan about 5 minutes before removing.

Food Is Medicine

TYRA LANE-KINGSLAND

. . . .

It flowed down the center of the main street. On each side of the river grew a tree of life, bearing twelve crops of fruit, with a fresh crop each month. The leaves were used for medicine to heal the nations.

Revelation 22:2 NLT

Whether it's the favored starting course to your meal or relegated as an afterthought pushed to the side, salad has long been a staple around the globe. Romans and ancient Greeks ate salad as greens mixed with oil and salt. In fact, that's where salad gets its name. The Latin term *herba salata* means "salted herb."

Salad often gets a bad rap. It's sometimes called "rabbit food" or "bird food." People crack jokes about it, remarking that women on dates only want to order a salad. But there's much to be said about this mighty meal item. A salad isn't merely iceberg, ranch, and croutons. There's tremendous taste, nutrients, and healing power available in a salad.

In today's verse, the apostle John gives us a hopeful promise. In this final chapter of the final book of the Bible, we are provided a glimpse of a restored Eden. And while this is a picture of what's to come, there is great truth we can mine from it for today. In verse 2 we see that plants are medicine. John describes the leaves on the trees being used to heal the nations.

In God's divine wisdom, he has shown me how to be a good steward over my health. He gave me deep insight as I embraced the truth of his Word from 1 Corinthians 6:19–20, which says, "Do you not know that your bodies are temples of the Holy Spirit, who is in you, whom you have received from God?

You are not your own; you were bought at a price. Therefore honor God with your bodies." Part of the plan God gave me for stewarding my health was to eat a salad a day. Following that plan has enabled me to stay healthy and strong throughout six pregnancies, has supported me in maintaining a healthy weight, and helps me have sharp, clear thinking throughout my day.

With so many differing eating modalities promoted today, one thing that most seem to agree on is the benefits of eating vegetables. While eating trends come and go, eating the good of the earth is not a novel idea. One of God's first gifts to humankind was to provide what would be for our bodily nourishment. In the very beginning, he placed us in a garden and said, "I give you every seed-bearing plant on the face of the whole earth and every tree that has fruit with seed in it. They will be yours for food" (Gen. 1:29).

In God's infinite creativity, he designed a bounty not only pleasing to the palate but restorative to the body. From the vibrant hues of rainbow Swiss chard to the mineral rich tender petals of spinach, the leaves on the trees have the power to fight free radicals and fortify the body. Even Popeye the Sailor Man, a cartoon character first seen in the late 1920s, drew his strength from eating spinach. Not just in comics but in real life, plants have that kind of power. These words often credited to Hippocrates, "Let food be thy medicine and medicine be thy food," echo what God has already shown us in his Word. May we partake of God's vast garden and walk in radiant health.

GRILLED PEACH SALAD

Recipe from 30 Days 30 Ways to Salad Heaven *by Tyra Lane-Kingsland.* *

Serves 2

For the salad

1 peach, halved and pitted
1 tsp olive oil
4 cups green leaf lettuce

1 Tbs chopped shallot
2 Tbs crumbled goat cheese
2 Tbs chopped pecans

1. Lightly oil the cut side of each peach half (or lightly spray with an oil mister). Grill peaches for 5 minutes over medium-high heat.

2. Divide remaining salad ingredients between two plates, drizzle with balsamic dressing, and top each with a grilled peach half.

For the balsamic vinaigrette

1 Tbs balsamic vinegar
⅓ cup olive oil
1 clove garlic, finely minced
½ tsp maple syrup

½ tsp dried rosemary
⅛ tsp salt
⅛ tsp pepper

Place vinaigrette ingredients in a glass jar, cover securely, and shake until well combined.

* Tyra Lane-Kingsland, *30 Days 30 Ways to Salad Heaven* (self-published, 2023), ebook, available at https://inspiredfullyshop.square.site/product/30days30waystosaladheaven/9.

The Ingredients of a Memory

True Friendship

AMY NEMECEK

. . . .

Friends love through all kinds of weather, and families stick together in all kinds of trouble.

Proverbs 17:17 Message

My mother died in the summer of 1993. I had just finished my freshman year of college, and I felt completely lost. Thirty years later, and there are days when I still do.

Through the decades, I've stayed in touch with Mom's best friend, Joanne, who has been an auntie to me my whole life. She's getting older, but we enjoy having coffee together and making the occasional short trip to Amish country in Shipshewana, Indiana. She faithfully prays for me every day because my mom isn't here to do that.

During my childhood, Aunt Jo and Mom would call each other nearly every day and swap recipes and prayer requests and parenting tips. Now she and I call each other every other week or so. It's always good to hear her voice as we update each other on family news and talk about what books we're reading.

Recently, Aunt Jo called me late on a Sunday afternoon. I had talked to her only a few days earlier, so when I heard her voice I worried something was wrong.

"Hi, Auntie. Is everything okay?"

"Hi, honey," she said. "Everything's fine. I was just thinking about your mom. Tomorrow would have been her birthday, you know."

I knew. I'd been thinking about Mom, too, and missing her like always. There was a pause as I felt a lump rise in my throat. Aunt Jo continued.

"I sure do miss her. We could talk about anything and everything. She was such a good friend, a bright light in my life, and I will not forget her. I just wanted you to know I'm remembering her today and missing her with you."

I will forever treasure that phone call. She and Mom had made such an impact on each other's lives that here, thirty years on, Aunt Jo still felt the absence of that friendship. It reminded me of this verse from the book of Psalms: "Those who are righteous will be long remembered" (112:6 NLT).

One of my favorite desserts to bake, whether it's for a family gathering or small group or church potluck, is a recipe Aunt Jo sent me years ago when I was living in a new place and missing my family back in West Michigan. Making it somehow helped me feel closer to the place I always knew as home—and it's even tastier in late July when I can use fresh, sweet, plump Michigan berries that I pick myself. I call it best friends blueberry buckle, and when it's in the oven, the house smells amazing!

Proverbs 27:9 says, "The sweet smell of incense can make you feel good, but true friendship is better still" (CEV). The gracious fragrance of the special bond shared by my mom and her best friend still wafts through the rooms of my life. Friendships like that are so rare these days, but I think it's something we all long for deep down.

I've heard people talk about a "2:00 a.m. friendship," the kind where you can call each other in the middle of the night and not be mad that you were woken up. That kind of friendship is special. But even better, I think, is a "blueberry buckle friendship," the kind where two friends make such a difference in each other's lives that the sweet aroma of grace carries down through decades to bless their children and grandchildren long after they are gone.

That's the true friendship my mom shared with her best friend. And that's the true friendship I want to model for others.

BEST FRIENDS BLUEBERRY BUCKLE

Serves 12

¼ cup butter, softened
¾ cup sugar
1 egg
1 cup milk

2 cups flour
2 tsp baking powder
½ tsp salt
2 cups fresh blueberries

Streusel topping

½ cup sugar
⅓ cup flour

¼ cup cold butter, cubed
½ tsp cinnamon

1. Preheat oven to 350°. Grease the bottom and sides of a 7×11 baking dish. In a mixing bowl, cream together butter and sugar. Add egg and milk and mix until thoroughly combined. In a separate bowl, sift together flour, baking powder, and salt, then add to the wet ingredients and mix just until combined. Carefully fold in the blueberries. Spread batter in the prepared baking dish.

2. For the topping, combine sugar, flour, butter cubes, and cinnamon in a small mixing bowl and mix until it has the texture of coarse breadcrumbs. Sprinkle the topping evenly over the batter.

3. Bake for 40–45 minutes until edges are browned. Remove pan to wire rack and allow to cool. Cut into 12 squares and share with friends!

Joy in the Dumplings

CINDY K. SPROLES

. . . .

Consider it pure joy, my brothers and sisters, whenever you face trials of many kinds.
James 1:2

Cold or hot. It doesn't matter. I love chicken and dumplings. Thanks to my grandmother, they are my go-to comfort food.

I spent a lot of summer days with my grandmother. Her small farm housed two cows, a pig, an entire host of chickens, and a small garden we planted yearly. Everything at Grandma's house was hard work, and everything had a purpose. It was her provision. Born in 1900, she never worked outside her four-room home, but she cared, loved, and cooked for everyone.

In her seventies, Grandma wasn't afraid of work. She was outside daily, tending something, before the rooster crowed. By midmorning, she dripped with perspiration. Still, Grandma never complained. There was always a song on her lips.

When I stayed with her, she'd roll me out of bed early. I'd wash up and set the table, and she'd serve me chicken and dumplings depending on her mood. On a hot summer morning, they'd be cold. When the cool dampness of fall hung in the air, the dumplings would be piping hot.

Chicken and dumplings landed on her table for breakfast, lunch, or supper. Regardless of when, how many times, or whether the circumstance was good or bad, when Grandma made that wonderful delight, she never failed to make it with joy. Her life was hard, and though Grandma knew she had no control over her circumstances, she did have control over how she approached the situation. She chose to do that with joy.

James opens his letter with this tough challenge. It's important to understand what he doesn't say. He doesn't tell us to be happy about all the bad things that happen. Instead, we should count each trial as a reason to rejoice—an opportunity to grow, to know Christ deeper, and to be stronger in our dependence on the Father. He isn't referring to a sudden emotional response that happens when we're thrown into difficulties. Instead, James teaches us how to label these moments when we compare them to our lives as a whole. How will these hardships make us stronger? That is the pure joy James refers to.

One fall, the bank insisted on an additional house payment from my grandmother. I will never forget her stance in the bank—arms behind her back, head bowed slightly. She stood in thought, pondering her words. I watched as her mouth moved silently. After a few moments, she looked the banker in the eye and spoke aloud. "Well, there is no more money, so I guess I'll churn double the butter. In the meantime, chicken and dumplings are on the table at supper. I'll have a place set for you and the Mrs. I won't take no for an answer." The stunned banker stared as my grandmother scribbled her address on a piece of paper. She pressed it against his chest and smiled. "Don't you be late." Then Grandma spun around on her heel, took me by the hand, and out the door we went—her humming all the way home.

As she worked to make her dumplings, she whistled and sang.

"Grandma, aren't you upset?" I asked.

"I'm not thrilled, but this hiccup will make me better. Besides, the Lord always cares for his children. Our job is to rejoice."

She was happy in her difficult situation. When suppertime rolled around, she set out a feast—green beans with ham bits, chicken and dumplings, mustard greens with vinegar, and mashed potatoes. The banker arrived, and Grandma welcomed him and his lovely wife into her home. We enjoyed a wonderful meal, and when the evening ended, the banker bought all the butter Grandma had churned plus a bushel of beans from her garden—enough money for her to make the extra payment.

Grandma taught me wonderful things happen around a meal prepared in joy. God grows us when our hardships are collected as deposits in our life's accounts. Every dumpling meal may not earn an extra bank payment, but it draws us closer to God. Count it all pure joy.

CHICKEN AND DUMPLINGS

Serves 4

For dumplings

2 cups flour

1 Tbs baking powder

½ cup milk or water (enough to make a tight dough)

For chicken

1 chicken, cut up (or two chicken breasts and thighs)

8 cups water

½ tsp each salt and pepper

½ cup butter (1 stick)

1 cup milk

1. Mix together flour and baking powder, then add enough water or milk to make a tight dough. Roll out dough on floured surface to about ¼ inch thick.

2. Meanwhile, bring chicken to a boil in the water and cook until tender. Remove chicken, and then add salt, pepper, and butter to broth.

3. Cut dough into strips about 1 inch wide and 4 inches long. Drop strips into the boiling broth. Cook for ten minutes, stirring lightly to help dumplings cook evenly (too much stirring breaks them down into starch). Add 1 cup milk and remove from heat. Add chicken back into the pot with the dumplings before serving.

4. Serve as is or over mashed potatoes. Good cold or hot.

Layers of Identity

JENNY ERLINGSSON

. . . .

I will remember the deeds of the LORD; yes, I will remember your miracles of long ago. I will consider all your works and meditate on all your mighty deeds.

Psalm 77:11–12

Plantain. Some hate it. Others love it. I find myself among the latter. For me, that love is about more than the crisp, slightly salty outer coating that gives way to a sweet tender center. More than the caramelized sugars and the tantalizing scent of roasted banana. It is the aroma of home. A fragrance more poignant now than before. A trigger back to a childhood of white rice with red stew, black-eyed peas boiled until they resembled mash, fish soup thick as gumbo. The odor of fried plantain was so strong it reached us before we got to my mother's front door. Or on special occasions, we'd smell the sweet, buttery crunch of chin-chin, or puff-puff, a larger, doughnutlike version. I also recall bean pudding called moi-moi, and fufu dipped into okra-filled fish stew. Often with a dish of fried plantain on the side.

I missed those foods the most when we moved to Iceland several years ago. Those intricacies of culture not so purely American because my upbringing was also rooted in my Nigerian origin. I love Alabama barbecue and beloved Chick-fil-A, but the cultural foods my mother mixed in with American cuisine were what my heart craved.

The first time I walked into Iceland's only African store, I grinned at the familiar sights welcoming me to a bit of home across the ocean. I may not have been surrounded by the scents of my mother's kitchen or that pan of oil she kept ever ready, but as I leaned over the boxes overflowing with imported plantain, I began my own ritual of remembrance. Tapping and observing each fruit to make a careful selection. Grabbing a few bags of the chip version to snack on during our drive back to our seaside village. Smiling at the packages of chin-chin and containers of palm oil and bottles of malt lining the shelves.

All these ingredients ready to form meals more tangible than a memory. To piece together another part of my family's identity, a beautiful reminder of where we come from and also who we are meant to be.

The Bible is full of stories where food serves as a cherished reminder, from Passover to Purim, from mourning to laughter. Ingredients piece together to form meals of remembrance. Layer upon layer of memory stacking up into markers of the journey, triggers of core memories.

Imagine the significance of those meals, anchored in covenant and command, set in the center of community—breaking bread over shared experiences. As pots were stirred and morsels melted on tongues, imagine the wounds mended, the burdens undone. The reminder to mourn what had been lost but also to rejoice in what had been gained. As tangible as the plates held and passed and pulled from and poured into.

Those traditions around food hold significance for us too. My mom brought those memories with her from her native Nigeria, a move that wasn't without struggle. For our family, following God's call across the Atlantic to Iceland didn't come without cost. But even in the bitter, the moments strung together are so sweet. Filling my kitchen with the fragrance of my efforts. The ones my Jesus calls worship as I pour that offering on his feet.

As the plantain ripens, my son waits in anticipation. He sniffs out the source when fresh slices hit the heated oil. Grabs a golden slice as soon as it leaves the pan. Ignores my warnings to let it cool. Bites into the crisp to get to the tender, savoring the sweet memories of Nana's kitchen across the sea, while I check on the roasting lamb from the land in which we are called to be.

From this kitchen, I pray deep remembrance forms for my kids. That the scent of vanilla triggers memories of our hands mixing batter for pancakes. Kneading dough for Southern biscuits, adding chocolate chips to muffin mix. Layer after layer of core memories within the meals of our cultural identity. Aromas and warmth and remembrance wrapped up in the food of family.

SWEET FRIED PLANTAIN

Plantains look like very large bananas. You will find them in the store looking very green. Many cultures eat them at that point—baked, boiled, and fried. But this recipe is going to make you wait. You need the plantains to ripen until they are yellow with black streaks or even darker and are soft/tender to the touch. By the way, DO NOT eat plantains raw. They are a starchy fruit meant to be cooked. Raw plantain may not be so fun for your stomach.

With hot, shallow oil needed, this is probably not a good recipe for kids to make with you. And I suggest keeping the pan away from an edge burner. Okay, on to the ingredients and directions!

Serves 6

2–4 ripe plantains
salt for sprinkling

oil for frying (olive, avocado, coconut, or other high-temp oil of choice; I use a light olive oil good for frying)

1. Peel each plantain by carefully cutting off each end and slicing the skin lengthwise just enough to peel the plantain, not cut through the flesh.

2. Once each plantain is peeled, slice into ⅓-inch circular or oval slices and place in a large bowl.

3. Pour oil into frying pan until it is about ½ to 1 inch deep and heat to medium-high heat.

4. From here, you can either toss the sliced plantains with a little salt before frying or sprinkle them with salt after you are finished. Or use no salt at all.

5. When the oil is hot but not smoking (oil should bubble on contact), carefully place slices in the pan one at a time with a fork or tongs. Depending on the size of your pan, you can fry 6–12 pieces at a time. Fry for 3–4 minutes or until golden brown around the edges. Then carefully flip the slices to fry the other side. Be careful not to splash the hot oil when you flip.

6. After the other side is ready, remove plantain from the pan, letting excess oil drip off, and place on a plate. If you want your plantain extra drained, put a mesh strainer over a bowl and then place the fried slices there before transferring to a plate.

Serving recommendation: enjoy this crispy-edged, caramelized goodness on its own or as a side with beans, rice, meat, whatever your heart desires. And if you like it enough, who knows what kind of core kitchen memory you'll form for your friends and family?

A Holiday to Remember

CONNIE CLYBURN

. . . .

This is the day that the LORD has made; let us rejoice and be glad in it.
Psalm 118:24 ESV

We thought we had a winner of an idea that Thanksgiving. My mom's sister had been battling health issues and wasn't able to cook for her family, so my mom and my uncle decided to cook a turkey with all the trimmings. It would be nice to have the family together, and what could possibly go wrong?

My mom wanted to do this for her sister, so she set about making plans. Several of us, including my husband and some of my cousins, gathered in my aunt and uncle's cozy home to try to help in the kitchen, or at least entertain everyone else while the cooking commenced. My mom assumed the role of head cook, giving her helpers jobs to prepare the meal. We reviewed our lists.

Turkey in the oven. Check.

Potatoes peeled and in the pot to boil. Check.

Green beans ready. Check.

Rolls in the bread pan. Check.

After some preparation, things seemed to be humming along in the kitchen. Delicious scents from the baking and cooking wafted through the air. Thanksgiving was moving full speed ahead. Soon we would all gather around the table to partake of a sumptuous meal prepared by loving hands. My cousins and I kept my aunt company in the living room. We laughed over old times and talked about the coming holidays and winter months that would follow.

Suddenly a commotion erupted in the kitchen. Everyone jumped up and ran that way to see flames coming from the oven—the turkey was on fire! Quick action brought the situation under control before the whole stove went up along with the bird. We fanned smoke through the open kitchen door and turned to take account of the devastation. I don't remember who was brave enough to peek inside to examine the turkey, but somebody did, and we declared it still edible—most of it, anyway.

All in all, I thought it turned out to be a good day. It would be my aunt's last Thanksgiving with us, but I remember it fondly. I tend to have a funny memory from most every family event, like the time my papaw got big red women's bloomers at a family Christmas celebration. (But that's another story for another time.)

Gatherings with my family are some of my favorite memories. It's not the food I look forward to so much as spending time with them. My cousins and I grew up close-knit, having summer sleepovers and riding our bikes down country lanes on our way to the local convenience store to get grape slushes.

My world has changed significantly over the years, as many of my family members have passed on. Our tables aren't as full now, and we don't get together like before. I miss those days, but I've also realized that I don't have to be sad over the loss of our big gatherings. I can look forward to even the simplest moments with family. I will create new memories, like sunny day picnics in the car with my mom and meeting at the local diner each week with other family members.

I believe that's what our heavenly Father wants us to do: cherish even the small moments of the day. So, instead of being sad over times I consider gone forever, I'll enjoy today and celebrate the little things.

Hands That Speak

NICOLA GORDON

. . . .

Behold, I have inscribed you on the palms of My hands.
Isaiah 49:16 NASB

My mother's hands speak. Every line, wrinkle, and age spot is a chapter in the storybook of her life. Many of these chapters tell of the years she devoted to mothering. With her hands she carried, hugged, comforted, nourished, protected, provided, cheered, celebrated, instructed, corrected, and prayed for my two siblings and me. Beautifully braided hair embellished with ribbons for my sister and me, a button restored to my shirt in time to catch the school bus, and a mixture of honey and lemon juice administered on a spoon for a sore throat are but a few of the stories of her hands.

A conversation of kitchen love was spoken regularly by my mother's hands. Freshly baked muffins that awaited our return from school, the best apple crisp, creatively shaped and decorated birthday cakes, and Sunday roast beef dinners still hang in the hallway of my memories. I treasure the times I was invited to partake in such a dialogue as this. As a young girl, I learned the art of rolling pie pastry while standing next to my mother equipped with the finest baker's tools: a tinfoil pie plate, a lump of playdough, and a rolling pin. What a brilliant teacher! However, my favorite hands-on lesson was learning to bake Christmas squares, in particular Mars squares. As the name may suggest, they are on a planetary level when it comes to taste. Yes, truly out of this world! With a buttery shortbread base, a caramel middle, and a thin chocolate topping, they are a very special treat our family reserved for Christmas.

This hand-to-hand language spoken alongside one another in the kitchen was a conduit for the passing on of skills and family traditions, building a mother-daughter relationship, and engaging in meaningful conversation.

Why is the language of a mother's hands so important, so necessary, so beautiful, and so effective? Because it is love spoken in action—*love demonstrated.* In Jesus's earthly ministry, he sometimes used his physical hands as an extension of God the Father to demonstrate his love and power to a watching world. His hands welcomed and blessed children (Mark 10:13–16), healed a man with a skin disease (1:40–41), broke loaves of bread to feed more than five thousand people (Matt. 14:19), and restored the sight of two blind men (9:27–30). Some seven centuries before the prophecy was fulfilled, Isaiah's words pointed to the most incredible, unmatchable, humanly unfathomable thing Jesus Christ would do as the ultimate demonstration of his love for humankind. Isaiah 49:16 reads: "Behold, I have inscribed you on the palms *of My hands*" (NASB, emphasis added). God took the initiative in demonstrating his love for us while we were in our sinful state through the willful sacrifice of his Son Jesus Christ on the cross (Rom. 5:8). Jesus's death paid the price to buy us back, thereby forgiving all our sins and reconciling us to him (Rom. 5:10; Eph. 1:7). *The hands of Jesus Christ nailed to the cross wrote the most powerful love story of God for his people!*

A godly mother seeks to imitate God in every aspect of her life because of the grace and love freely extended to her for the forgiveness of her sins at the cross (Eph. 5:1–2). This is the best thing she can endeavor to pass on to her children, not as a tradition or a seasonal event but as a pattern of life. My mother's hands have long ceased from the strivings of child-rearing years, but the one thing they will never stop speaking is the love of God. Mom continues to hold the Word of God in her hands daily and lets it speak into her heart and life.

What stories will our hands tell?

MARS SQUARES

Yields 48 squares

For the shortbread base

1 cup salted butter (2 sticks), slightly softened

½ cup white sugar

2 cups all-purpose flour

For the caramel filling

1 cup salted butter (2 sticks)

6 Tbs corn syrup

1 cup brown sugar

1 (14 oz) can sweetened condensed milk

For the chocolate topping

¾ cup semisweet chocolate chips (approx.)

1 tsp butter (approx.)

1. Preheat oven to 325°.

2. For the shortbread base, in a medium bowl, mix butter, white sugar, and all-purpose flour together. Then pat into a lightly greased 9×13 pan.

3. Using a fork, gently prick holes in the surface of the shortbread, being careful not to press in too deeply.

4. Bake for about 20 minutes, until the shortbread is lightly browned. Remove the pan from the oven and set aside.

5. Bring all ingredients for the caramel filling to a boil at medium heat while stirring *continuously*. Boil, while stirring, for 6 minutes.

6. Pour the filling over the shortbread base and allow to cool completely. When the pan has cooled, cover with plastic wrap and put it into the refrigerator to finish setting. You can leave it for a few hours or until the following day before completing it with the chocolate topping.

7. For the chocolate topping, combine chocolate chips and butter in a small, microwave safe bowl, covering it to avoid any splatter. Melt gradually, using intervals of 10–15 seconds and stirring after each, until mixture is fully melted and smooth. Stir until well blended and then spread in an even layer over the caramel filling.

8. With a small knife, lightly mark in the chocolate where you will complete the final cutting of the squares later. (For 48 squares, this means marking 5 lines [6 rows] down the short side and 7 lines [8 rows] down the long side.) Return the pan to the refrigerator until the chocolate sets. When the chocolate has set, allow the pan to come to room temperature for a few minutes before using a slightly wet knife to cut into squares. Enjoy right away or freeze for up to a month.

Dining in God's Creation

RACHEL MCRAE

. . . .

The heavens declare the glory of God; the skies proclaim the work of his hands.
Psalm 19:1

Many of us can recall childhood memories with certain tastes and smells. Whether it's our grandmother's key lime pie or our dad's excellent grilling skills, we can be transported to a moment in time with just a bite or the whiff of charcoal in the air.

Sometimes a trip or activity can bring to mind these culinary recollections as well. A hike in the woods could remind you of weeklong family camping trips where you ate food that you'd never eat any other time of the year, like sloppy joes and s'mores. Or beach vacations where you feasted on a bounty of seafood that was just as much of a treat as the double scoop of ice cream you'd have afterward (with sprinkles, of course).

I share a special food memory with a group of people who grew up attending and working at a summer camp in the mountains of East Tennessee. One night each week, we'd take the older campers out of the main camp and up a mountain for an overnight campout. We'd set up our tents, get the fires going, and then gather the ingredients for dinner. Each group was given a portion of hamburger, a handful of potatoes, onions, and carrots, a selection of condiments, a lot of aluminum foil, and a shovel. This was all we needed to make what we affectionately called Hobo Stew.

The kids from the city and suburbs would glance between the pile of ingredients, the raging campfire, and their counselors with a look that easily conveyed their skepticism about how all of this would work. Many would

121

start rummaging through their bags for the contraband they'd brought from the canteen because they knew there was a high chance that's all they'd be eating that night.

Then we'd gather our dubious campers and give each one a task. Some would chop the vegetables while others sprinkled salt and pepper on the meat. The ones fascinated with fire were in charge of manning the hot coals and getting the shovel ready. Once prepared, everything went into the aluminum foil, and one child with very clean hands would be allowed to mush everything up together before the foil was sealed into a packet. And into the fire the packet went.

Our new wilderness chefs were now on board with the meal that awaited. They chatted about all the things that were cooking and their role in making it happen. And when the packet was pulled out of the fire? You would have thought the biggest Thanksgiving turkey was laid in front of them with the amount of oohs and ahs that resonated from the group. They were very impressed with their creation and ready to dive in.

Eating Hobo Stew under a starry sky was certainly a highlight of each camper's week. The community that was built around our outdoor kitchen created memories and opened young hearts and minds to God's beautiful creation and all he fills it with.

Decades later, when I think of my summers in the mountains, I always think of Hobo Stew, as I know other camp alumni do. Several of us recently had a camp reunion via social media where we cooked Hobo Stew from our homes all around the country. Pictures and videos were shared of many of these same campers and counselors making the treasured recipe in their kitchens and backyards with their own families.

Cooking and dining outside can be a refreshing way to enjoy God's bounty in his provision of both food and fellowship. Grab some friends and create your own picnic site. Go camping and try cooking on a camp stove or open fire. Or simply take your dinner to the back porch for a change in scenery. Wherever you choose to dine, be grateful for the many blessings that surround you through friends, family, and creation.

HOBO STEW

Serves 4

1½ lbs ground beef
4 russet potatoes, peeled and
  sliced very thin
2–3 med carrots, sliced
2 yellow onions, sliced

1 cup ketchup (plus a bit more if you
  want more sauce)
½ cup yellow mustard
salt and pepper to taste

1. Mix all of the ingredients together well in a large bowl.

2. Take two sheets of heavy aluminum foil, about 24 inches each, and lay them out on the counter with the long sides overlapping. Put mixture in the center of the foil and spread out into a log shape. Add four ice cubes to the packet for added moisture.

3. Wrap the mixture up tightly in the foil (make the packet flat versus thick) and close the ends up.

If cooking in a conventional oven

1. Cook in a 450° oven for 45–50 minutes (if packet is too thick, it could take up to an hour).

2. Slice packet open carefully with a knife and serve.

If cooking in a firepit

1. Let a fire burn long enough to get a lot of hot coals. You'll need the coals to cook, not flaming logs. Double wrap the packet in heavy-duty foil. Rake a few coals to the side, place your packet in the coals, and rake some coals over the top of the packet. Cook in the firepit for about 20–25 minutes.

2. Remove from pit with a shovel, being careful not to tear the packet. Carefully slice open the packet with a knife and serve.

A Taste of the Holidays

JENNIFER DRUMMOND

. . . .

Everyone will share the story of your wonderful goodness; they will sing with joy about your righteousness.

Psalm 145:7 NLT

My eyes barely reached the top of the glass bowl. The scalloped edge dipped and rose, beautiful cups hanging around the rim. I lowered my head to watch the creamy apricot line rise, small bubbles swirling around, as Aunt Laurie added the club soda to the punch. She dumped the last bit in with a flourish and a singsong "Ta-da!" I was mesmerized by the generous layer of fizz, and a tingle of excitement bubbled within me. "David," she called. "You're up!"

Uncle Dave came around the corner, a giant tub of orange sherbet in his arms. *Thhhwwwppptttt*—he pulled open the plastic lid, laying the circle next to me. He held back a smile, but his eyes sparkled as I swiped a tiny bit of the frozen treat. His strong hand gripped the silver ice cream scooper, and I watched as orange clouds of sherbet began floating in the sea of apricot foam. I couldn't wait for my own glass, a special treat made only on Christmas Day.

Years later, my mother was downsizing in preparation for a move to Florida, and she offered me her crystal punch bowl. I traced the edge of it with my finger, triangles instead of scalloped curves to hold the twelve finely decorated glasses from the rim. Memories of my cousins and me gathered around waiting to make the punch flooded back. I could feel that tingle of excitement, waiting for the sherbet to be added. Imagining my future children gathered around, peering into the wonder of an apricot-colored Christmas delight, I couldn't wait for them to share in that magic. But my sweet reverie was interrupted by my husband's voice: "We're not taking *that* giant thing, are we?" After some vigorous discussion, an admittedly big box was packed, and for fifteen years, that crystal punch bowl moved with us six times. We never even unpacked it.

But once we finally settled into our own home, the crystal bowl did come out of the box and with us to our friends' house for Christmas dinner. The punch was a big hit, with kids and adults alike enjoying a fancy glass full of the fizzy drink, sipping a scoopful of the sweet sherbet. Absurdly pleased at everyone's enjoyment, I carried that feeling of connection well into the new year. The following Christmas found us together again, preparing and sharing the punch over conversation and celebration. However, it was the third year when the magic happened.

I pulled out the large bowl, and all the children gathered around. The youngest of the gaggle carefully hung the beautiful glasses all around the rim, guided by my oldest. Her brother helped open the jar of apricot nectar, and we used the can opener to poke the necessary triangular holes in the pineapple juice can. My son and I poured the club soda together, watching the creamy line rise up the side of the bowl. I ended with a flourishing "Ta-da!" and called to my husband, "You're up." He came around the corner, a tub of sherbet in his strong arms. Using the silver ice cream scooper, he plopped beautiful orange mounds into the bowl. I watched one of our other little onlookers, who was himself watching the process, and felt a familiar tingle of excitement. "I can't wait for a glass," he murmured.

When his mom called me the next day and told me that he'd said, "That punch tastes like Christmas," I knew just what he meant.

As you reflect on the traditions passed down to you, are there particular ones for which you are grateful? As you consider your current life, are there celebrations you would like to invest in? As you ponder your legacy, in what ways do you want to bless future generations?

AUNT LAURIE'S PUNCH

Yields 2 large punch bowls

1 jar (33 oz) apricot nectar (can
  substitute mango juice)
1 can (46 oz) pineapple juice

2 liters club soda (or plain seltzer water)
1 gallon orange sherbet

1. Mix half of the apricot nectar and half of the pineapple juice together in a large serving bowl.

2. Add half of the club soda—slowly. Then carefully add scoopfuls of orange sherbet until you've used half of it.

3. When serving, use a ladle to scoop some punch, including a mound of sherbet in each cup.

4. Repeat steps to make the second batch of punch using the remaining ingredients.

Mud Magic

CHAD R. ALLEN

. . . .

"All we have are five loaves of bread and two fish," they said. . . . He took the five loaves and two fish, lifted his face to heaven in prayer, blessed, broke, and gave the bread to the disciples. The disciples then gave the food to the congregation. They all ate their fill. They gathered twelve baskets of leftovers. About five thousand were fed.

Matthew 14:17–21 Message

In 1979, my mom and I lived in a small, light green, ranch-style house on McConnell Air Force Base just south of Wichita, Kansas. I was about four years old, and it was a spring morning after a night of heavy rain. Just to the side of the front steps, I'd found some of the most delightful mud a child could get their hands into. That's where I was, mussed red hair, legs pale as paper, hunched over, clearly doing something very important.

I was absorbed in my task, creating mud pies about the size of my palms. Musty coolness filled my nose as I grabbed each handful, slapped it into shape, and carefully placed it in an old shoebox Mom gave me. The job took the better part of an hour, I imagine, and then it was time for lunch.

I brought my treasures to Mom, who somehow had the composure not to freak out about fresh mud making its way through her front door. Instead, her eyes grew wide with what seemed—to me, at least—like pride and wonder. I had a hunch these were splendid objects of beauty, and her response settled it. I had done something remarkable.

She quickly took the box and placed it "for safekeeping" on the counter by the fridge, and we had lunch together. Then it was time for my nap.

Later that afternoon, I came back into the kitchen to see how my mud pies were getting on. I thought maybe they'd be hard, and I could go chuck them against the driveway. But when I pulled the box down from the counter and removed the lid, this time it was my turn for wide eyes.

What lay inside that box was no longer mud but freshly baked chocolate chip cookies!

The awe I felt in that moment, it occurred to me years later, must have been similar to what the disciples felt when they brought a shoebox of food to Jesus—when he turned around and used it to feed thousands of people.

God can do magic with our mud. All we have to do is bring it to him.

Seasoning That Lasts

KIT TOSELLO

. . . .

Start children off on the way they should go, and even when they are old they will not turn from it.

Proverbs 22:6

As a mom to three adult children, I'm sometimes haunted by a specific worry. While they were under my roof, had I neglected to add all the best ingredients in just the perfect quantity? Of course I had. Of course I fell short. So I'll sometimes wrestle with my pillow at night, conjuring up ways to sneak in a bit more instruction. Extra seasoning.

Never mind that they haven't asked for it.

These fears evaporate whenever I fill our kitchen with the savory aroma of what my parents called Spanish rice. A staple of my growing-up years, this comforting dish is much more than its name implies. Think of it as stuffed bell peppers, deconstructed.

When I was young, our long galley kitchen was where my father and I intersected most often. We were both late-night squirrels, midnight snacking together in that kitchen with its yellow-tiled countertops and harvest gold appliances. Also, Dad sometimes cooked dinner for the family. When he did, he rocked it like a pro.

One evening, Spanish rice was on the menu.

"How'd you learn to cook?" I must have asked. My dad was a college teacher, not a chef.

"Help me chop these onions," he probably said. "And I'll tell you."

As I complied, Dad regaled me with long-ago stories of selling Revere cookware door-to-door. He was an outgoing and enthusiastic man with laughing eyes, so I don't doubt his success in persuading people to invite him into their homes. Once inside, he became a Guy Fieri, flashing mad cooking skills learned from Revere as he prepared a family meal with shiny Revere pots and pans. Cookware they could now own!

Dad must have noticed me struggling with the knife. He came up behind me, encircled me in his arms, and curled the fingers of my left hand into proper position. I'm sure he smelled of Belair cigarettes and Folgers coffee. "Keep the blade firm, up against your knuckles, like this," he instructed. "Or we'll be serving fingertip soup for supper."

Next came bright green bell peppers. Dad demonstrated how to scrape out the seeds and chop them coarsely, releasing their sweet fragrance.

When I prepare Spanish rice today, I substitute ground turkey for ground beef, use cauliflower rice instead of long grain white. Still, the smell of simmering onion and garlic, bell pepper and diced tomatoes, punctuated with cumin and a pinch of chili pepper, transports me back to that yellow galley kitchen. I feel Dad's arms around me, hear his gravelly smoker's voice, see his teasing eyes sparkle.

My father didn't live long enough to fret over his adult kids. Never had to face the temptation to keep drilling home in my adulthood the things he taught me in my childhood. Instead he fought cancer through my teen years and graduated to heaven the same year I graduated from high school.

Yet now, decades later, whenever I make Spanish rice, he's here in the kitchen with me. I'm reminded to be a friendly neighbor, like he was. Every time I press the knife blade up against my curled knuckles, I'm reminded to approach life with humor, enthusiasm, and faith. Like he did. And as the aroma of cumin mingles with garlic and bell pepper and tomatoes, this final lesson from my father's life and death seasons my mind and heart: I need not waste these precious days worrying whether I got everything right while my kids were young. That dish, by and large, is done. Whatever ingredients I infused into my children—wisdom, faith, safety with sharp objects—will long outlast me.

I can trust God that it'll do.

These days I see my father's enthusiasm alive and well in my grown son. His tender wisdom displayed in my oldest daughter. His playfulness shining through my youngest daughter's eyes.

And as for me, I've yet to slice a finger.

SPANISH RICE

Low-carb, keto-friendly

Serves 6

1 lb ground turkey or lean ground beef	1 rounded tsp ground cumin
1 lg yellow onion, chopped	1 tsp Italian herbs
2 lg green bell peppers, chopped	½ tsp chili powder
2 cloves garlic, minced	½ tsp onion powder
1 (14.5 oz) can diced fire-roasted tomatoes	1 lb frozen cauliflower rice
1 (8 oz) can tomato sauce	salt and pepper to taste

1. In large skillet, cook meat, onion, pepper, and garlic until meat is fully browned and vegetables are tender. Break up meat into crumbles. Drain if needed.

2. Stir in diced tomatoes (with their liquid) and tomato sauce. Add seasonings and bring to a simmer. Allow to simmer gently for several minutes so flavors develop.

3. Add cauliflower rice. Adjust seasonings as desired. Allow mixture to thoroughly reheat before serving.

Options

Add ¾ cup additional chopped vegetables (such as zucchini or yellow squash) during step 1. Before serving, stir in sliced olives, lime juice, chopped fresh cilantro, and/or diced green chiles. Serve with sour cream, shredded cheese, and/or sliced green onions.

A Delicious Memory

ANDREA DOERING*

. . . .

So I commend the enjoyment of life, because there is nothing better for a person under the sun than to eat and drink and be glad. Then joy will accompany them in their toil all the days of the life God has given them under the sun.

Ecclesiastes 8:15

A favorite children's book of mine is *The Search for Delicious* by Natalie Babbitt. The main quest is that of a king's page to find the true definition of *delicious*. In the process, he encounters a farmer who, in front of everyone including his wife, asserts the quest need go no further—*delicious* is defined by his mother's plum cake. That must be some cake, I've always thought, if you're willing to risk domestic harmony as well as be assured your wife will now never make you a plum cake.

Jack, my father-in-law, had a similar reverie about his mother's plum cake. He also spoke about it in front of his wife. What is it about plum cake that causes grown men to become culinary traitors? I'd never had one, but it seemed a good idea to know what I was missing. I decided to try to make one, and I enlisted my in-laws' help as testers.

My first attempt was a flat affair, but I'd included what Jack told me—it had to be absolutely chock-full of very ripe plums, and they had to be Italian plums. These are the fresh, oblong-shaped ones. The cake smelled delicious, but did it deliver the taste of memories, of mothers and ripe plums and the long summer days of youth? I called my in-laws, told them not to

* Adapted from Andrea Doering, *The Children's Table: Recipes and Meals Inspired by Favorite Children's Stories* (Waite Park, MN: Sandalwood Press, 2014).

order dessert when they went out, and then delivered the still-warm cake to their kitchen.

The next day my mother-in-law called, and announced, "Your cake was *delicious!*"

I had to smile—the word we were looking for. Then I asked, "Now, did it taste like the one Jack's mom used to make?"

Her answer was just as swift and sure. "Oh, no. You didn't use yeast."

Yeast? Apparently I was going to be trying again. I called my sister. "She says it needs yeast. Have you ever heard of a cake with yeast?" She thought for a moment, riffling through her compendium of knowledge.

"I have a recipe for Italian cake that uses yeast. I think they use it in place of baking powder. It's really good, and maybe you could modify it. I'll send it to you."

She did. We decided this second attempt was like an Italian version of pound cake, and the result certainly met my own search for *delicious*. The plums were this nice surprise in the bottom of the cake; the cake was high and yet dense and lemony. I called my in-laws again. "Don't order dessert. I've got version two coming over."

It was a week before I could reconnect with them, and I was eager to ask if we'd hit upon the right mix. Was it like the cake Jack's mother made?

They collectively shook their heads, though in hindsight they didn't look too sad or reluctant to deliver the news. "No, the first one was more like it. It's very thin—you make it on a cookie sheet. And you use yeast."

It made me wonder how many more plum cakes I would have to make before I got all the ingredients and instructions out of them. Or is this just how our memory works? We keep fitting the key in the lock, and each time we get a bit further, and only when the taste and our memory hit a disconnect do we realize there was more to it.

Version three involved borrowing a rimmed cookie sheet, buying more plums, and varying the first recipe to add yeast. And it was, according to my taste testers, *delicious*.

It was the best I could do because here's the truth: there is always more to it than the taste. The cake of Jack's memory, like the cake in *The Search for*

Delicious, was made by his mother. But my efforts were a way to reconnect time and love and memory, to bring it into the present day by means of a plum cake. It was a way for me to connect in a different way with my in-laws, and to celebrate with them a beautiful piece of their past.

PLUM CAKE

You will need a kitchen scale for this.

Serves 12

3 eggs
sugar
flour
½ cup butter (1 stick), melted

2¼ tsp yeast (1 packet)
1 lb Italian plums, halved and pitted
cinnamon and sugar

1. Preheat oven to 350°.

2. Weigh 3 eggs, still in their shells, making note of their weight.

3. Crack eggs into a mixing bowl and add the same weight of the eggs in sugar. Beat well, till fluffy and light—about a minute with an electric mixer. Add the same weight in flour and mix well.

4. In a separate bowl, combine yeast and melted butter, mixing well. Stir the butter/yeast mixture into the batter until well combined.

5. Grease and flour a rimmed 9x13x1 baking sheet and pour batter into it. Then place plums in the batter cut side up—you want to absolutely fill the baking sheet so the batter really is just a "grout" for a beautiful mosaic of plums.

6. Sprinkle with cinnamon and sugar and bake for about 35 minutes, or until cake does not stick to a toothpick or knife when tested and is golden brown.

The Presence of Love

ALYSSA ROGGIE ALLEN

· · · ·

Where can I go from your Spirit? Where can I flee from your presence? If I go up to the heavens, you are there; if I make my bed in the depths, you are there.

Psalm 139:7–8

I can't remember a holiday dinner that didn't include my grandma's apple salad. Made with simple ingredients like chopped apples, grapes, walnuts, celery, and a sweet dressing, you wouldn't think it would shine. It's no turkey, mashed potatoes, or homemade apple pie.

And yet, it's always the star of the table.

My dad, who is eighty-four, remembers eating it when he was a child. I remember eating it as a child. And now my children eat it and help make it.

That's four generations.

My grandma was a woman of deep faith. It permeated every facet of her being. She was a Mennonite, and I never saw her wear pants. She always wore her head covering. She studied Scripture faithfully and had a deep prayer life. She gave of her time and resources, baking bread for auctions to raise money for church camps and other causes. She cared for and lived off the earth, earning her family's income from a farm, raising much of their food in a massive garden, canning, making maple syrup, and more.

Most of the time, my life feels very distant from hers. Though we share a deep faith, mine seems more complicated than hers. Less rooted in simple, daily practices that carve out quiet, peace, and contentment. Less tied to God's provision through the earth (most of my family's food comes from a supermarket). Less reliant on a community of believers who support and sustain one another.

But not when I'm making apple salad.

Then, she's there.

I can feel her in my kitchen. I see her testing the dressing by dipping her pinkie finger in for a taste.

I can see her peeling the apples. How did she get the peel off all in one strip and waste so little of the fruit?

I can hear her singing a hymn while she cooked.

I can feel her wrinkled and arthritic hands around the cut crystal serving bowl, which I now use to serve the salad at my table.

Along with her presence, I somehow also feel closer to God. How is it possible that in chunks of apple, slices of celery, and dashes of vanilla, God infuses my soul? And in what other things—and people—is God revealing his Spirit to me every day, if only I stopped to notice?

GRANDMA ROGGIE'S APPLE SALAD

Serves 8

For the dressing

1 cup water
1 cup sugar
1–1½ Tbs flour
1 egg

3 Tbs butter
1 Tbs white vinegar
1 tsp vanilla

For the salad

6–7 med apples, peeled and diced
celery, diced

red grapes, halved
walnuts, chopped

1. For dressing, boil water in a small saucepan.

2. In a separate bowl, mix sugar, flour, and egg together. Pour mixture into boiling water and stir until smooth and thick.

3. Take off the heat and add butter, vinegar, and vanilla. Set aside to cool (dressing can be made the day before and refrigerated overnight).

4. Before serving, pour over apples. Add in celery, grapes, and walnuts (amounts to your preference).

The Ngorongoro Thanks Giving

LISA LARSEN HILL

• • • •

How good and pleasant it is when God's people live together in unity!

Psalm 133:1

My husband and I visited Tanzania many years ago. One of our first stops was the Ngorongoro Crater, which is called the Noah's ark of Africa because of the abundance of wildlife there. By a quirk of fate, a party of four that was supposed to be in our tour group never arrived. As a result, we had our private guide and driver, Calvin, the whole time. On our first night there, we arrived at the group camp and had a multigenerational family of ten join us at dinner. However, the second night we had the camp all to ourselves.

On that night, we enjoyed a refreshing drink on the rim of the crater. My husband, Roger, broke out our iPod and battery-operated speaker so we could listen to opera as we watched the last of the sun's rays. One of the kitchen crew approached to refresh our drinks. His name was Kito, which means "jewel." His name was fitting. He gazed at the speaker and listened to the music. He'd seen nothing like that before. He was only seventeen and told us he wanted to be the best dancer at the disco, all the while staring intensely at the speaker. Roger switched the playlist to some Johnny Cash, and Kito started singing along.

As evening closed in, we moved into the dining room tent, where we joined our driver, Calvin. We asked if the kitchen crew, who traditionally sat separately behind a curtain, could join us. He suggested giving them time to themselves. Before we knew it, though, Kito came out and asked if he could choose a song on the iPod. We smiled and agreed. He dialed up Shania Twain. With a nod from Calvin, we invited the kitchen crew to join us. They knew all the words to her songs and started singing and dancing.

Kito was the coolest cat in town. I jumped up and asked him if he knew how to swing dance. He didn't, but I offered to show him, and the group formed a circle around us. He was a quick learner, and his smile lit up the tent. His fellow crew clapped and howled with delight as we danced. The manager, a man much older than anyone else on the crew, also came from behind the curtain wearing a fancy hat, and he burst into the center of the dance circle, strutting his stuff, showing some amazing moves. It was obvious his employees had never seen him so expressive and relaxed. They clapped louder, cheering their leader on.

I had visions of animals gathering outside of the tent, swaying in the breeze as hyenas, elephants, and giraffes listened to the music. It was magical. There was no American or African, White or Black, guest or crew. We were all one. We lived in unity for a moment, enjoying each other's company.

With the angst in our world today, can we seek our commonalities rather than our differences? Can we celebrate our uniqueness together? There were three perspectives at that dinner. The crew appreciating their boss in a whole new light. The crew enjoying guests joining them in a jubilant way. And my husband and I delighted in experiencing a giving of thanks for such a magical interaction with new friends.

Indeed, "How good and pleasant it is when God's people live together in unity!" May you find opportunities to find harmony with your neighbors near and far.

At the end of the trip, we left our speaker behind as a gift to the kitchen crew. An unforgettable evening at the Ngorongoro Thanks Giving.

The Fruit of Her Hands

MARIANNE SHEHATA

· · · ·

And do not forget to do good and to share with others, for with such sacrifices God is pleased.

Hebrews 13:16

Mama. Mama Love. Mama's Food. Mama Magz. So many people love her, and they haven't even met my mama. "Send your mom a hug," they tell me. "Tell your mom I said hi." "Let her know I'll save her a piece of carrot cake next time I make it." Cards for Mama, flowers for Mama. Small tokens of gratitude for a home-cooked meal.

Mama loves to cook for people, and somehow her meals always land in the homes of people who need a warm hug. Maybe it is a tired mom with a new baby who is sick herself, a friend recovering from cancer, or a new immigrant who doesn't have enough money to cook a healthy meal. Somehow, Mama's food just has this way of finding people who need it the most. She sends scrumptious dishes, savory or sweet. Gifts of the earth that are transformed into waves of love and received on tantalized taste buds.

When we were growing up, one way Mama made us feel special was through her food. She worked very long, hard hours and was constantly on her feet, but she refused to ever use canned food, takeout, or frozen TV dinners. Each day, we had a warm and healthy meal. Mama also showed us love through special treats on our birthdays. Every year she would make each of her little girls a gourmet birthday cake for our parties. The cakes were always decorated beautifully and looked like they belonged in a fancy bakery. It was always the highlight of the birthday party, and I still remember our little hands and faces covered with chocolate buttercream icing. And who can forget Mama's decadent brownies? Or her famous Easter and Christmas cookies? The list continues. . .

The psalmist encourages us to "Taste and see that the LORD is good" (Ps. 34:8), to draw near to Christ and experience his goodness. In many ways, I feel Mama tangibly lives out this verse through the fruit of her hands. Not only is she a remarkable cook but she always makes her food with a great deal of love. When people eat her creations, they feel loved, remembered, and cherished. Often, when they call her to express their gratitude, she will say, "Thanks be to God!" They taste her food and feel her love, but ultimately they are reminded of the God who loves them beyond measure and has gone before them to provide for their needs.

Mama's cooking reminds me that a home-cooked meal provides strength to our bodies and also to our souls. As you prepare this dish, take time to think about and love the people you'll be feeding. I guarantee the food will taste even more delicious.

MAMA LOVE MIXED VEGGIE CASSEROLE

Recipe from Magda Shehata.

Serves 4–6

1 lg black eggplant (optional)
3 sm green zucchini
2 cups sliced onion
4 cloves garlic, finely chopped
3 bouillon cubes, crushed into a coarse powder (or 1 Tbs bouillon paste)
2 lg white or gold potatoes, diced
2 cups frozen peas
2 cups green beans, stemmed

3 med red tomatoes, cut into ½-inch slices
2 carrots, cut into ¼-inch slices
½ bottle (330 mL) strained tomatoes
2 cups water
1 Tbs honey
3 Tbs olive oil (and more for a drizzle here and there)
salt and pepper

Part A: Cutting and preparing vegetables

1. If using eggplant, peel and cut crosswise into 1-inch slices. Sprinkle with salt and let set for 1 hour in a colander to drain excess liquid.

2. Preheat oven to 425°.

3. Rinse eggplant to remove salt. Squeeze the pieces to remove moisture, then firmly pat with paper towels to dry.

4. Line a baking pan with parchment paper and place the eggplant slices on the pan. Drizzle generously with olive oil and bake about 30 minutes, until caramelized, turning once halfway through.

5. Peel zucchini and slice on the diagonal into ½-inch oval shapes. Put slices on a separate baking pan and drizzle with oil. Bake until very slightly roasted, approximately 5 minutes per side. It should be just tender to the touch.

6. Combine onions, garlic, and bouillon in a bowl and sprinkle with 1 tsp each salt and black pepper. Set aside. (Note: you can add your own additional flavorings at this time, such as dried oregano, basil, etc.)

Part B: Layering and baking

1. Reduce oven temp to 400°.

2. Put a layer of the onion and garlic mixture in the bottom of a large and deep baking dish.

3. Next, place a layer of sliced potato.

4. Alternate layers of onion and garlic mix with vegetables in the following order: green beans, onion mix, carrots, onion mix, peas, onion mix, zucchini, onion mix, eggplant, onion mix, and tomatoes.

5. In a separate bowl, combine tomato purée, water, 3 Tbs olive oil, honey, and salt and pepper to taste.

6. Pour this mixture on top of the vegetables and cover baking dish with foil.

7. Bake for 45 minutes, then remove foil and bake for another 15 minutes, until tomatoes look like sundried tomatoes and potatoes are tender.

8. Allow to rest for 20 minutes. Enjoy!

Lessons Learned in the Kitchen

Choose Your Own Adventure

LINDSEY SPOOLSTRA

. . . .

Jesus answered, "I am the way and the truth and the life. No one comes to the Father except through me."

John 14:6

One of my favorite things to make is hummus. It ticks all my boxes. It is simple to make, requires no great precision in either technique or measurements, tastes much better made from scratch and is healthier too, and has endless options for swapping out ingredients to use what I have on hand or match the particular flavor I'm craving.

I love options.

As a young reader, I was fond of the Choose Your Own Adventure series of books. The premise is simple: you begin reading the story, but after a short time, you're given a choice. In the book I remember best, your goal is to journey safely through a spooky forest. You turn the page and find the path divides. Do you go left or right? Choose right and turn to page 23, or choose left and turn to page 17. And so you make your choice and turn your page, and find out the consequences of your decision and what your next choice will be.

Maybe other (more modern?) books in the series are different, but that forest story had only one right path to safety, and many paths to, well, death.

I always seemed to get eaten by a giant tree. No matter which choices I made, I found myself sitting for just a minute to rest under its drooping branches and not waking up. I read the book so many times I could see it coming. I recognized page numbers and tried not to make choices that would land me there. I would use my fingers to keep as many pages open as possible, tracing my decision tree so I could backtrack and fix my mistakes if things didn't go well.

Hours of entertainment from one small paperback.

So on that note: Jesus.

I don't think I'm reaching too far to say that real life is also a choose your own adventure story in some ways. We might try to keep our fingers in the pages and backtrack our bad choices, and for sure the plotlines are much more complicated than death by hungry tree, but really—there's only one right path.

And yet this life is nothing like those books. It's not scripted. It might seem linear to us, but God is not bound by time or space as we are. The farther through the narrow gate we go, the wider our life in Christ gets. That one right path, rather than limiting our options, only leads us on and on, deeper and deeper, into greater possibilities.

The mysteries of God are vast and beyond human comprehension—but we're not told to keep our hands to ourselves or leave our brains at the door. No, we're invited to come right on in with all of ourselves—our minds, our bodies, our hearts—and all of our questions too. The gate is narrow, but once we're through, the way broadens endlessly. Jesus is the way, the truth, and the life, after all, and there's nothing small about him.

We come in, and we start with the basics. Then we grow. Develop. Explore. Accept that there will always be mystery. Paradox. More to discover. More to love.

If the book image doesn't do it for you, think of it like hummus: a simple recipe with endless variations that never gets old. I can't find a Scripture to back this up, but I feel in my heart that Jesus approves of hummus.

> Enter through the narrow gate. For wide is the gate and broad is the road that leads to destruction, and many enter through it. But small is the gate and narrow the road that leads to life, and only a few find it. (Matt. 7:13–14)

CHOOSE YOUR OWN ADVENTURE HUMMUS

Yields 2 cups

Classic Recipe

1½ cups cooked chickpeas, drained if
canned (liquid reserved)
2 Tbs lemon juice
2 cloves garlic

¼ cup tahini
¼–½ tsp salt
¼–½ tsp black pepper
2–4 Tbs olive oil

1. Combine all ingredients except olive oil in a food processor or blender and pulse a few times, then blend until ingredients come together, about 30 seconds or so. With the machine still running, drizzle in olive oil gradually until the hummus smooths out and reaches desired consistency. To reduce the oil, feel free to replace some or all of it with reserved liquid from the beans or with water. Taste and adjust seasoning as desired.

Got the basics down? Good. Now go forth and explore!

Roasted Garlic

Increase the garlic to 4–6 cloves and use the full 4 Tbs olive oil. Heat the oil in a small saucepan or skillet over medium-low heat; add cloves and sauté gently (oil should barely sizzle) until garlic is golden and softened, about 10 minutes. Proceed with base recipe as written.

Beet Beauty

Roast or steam 1 medium beet (8–10 oz) until softened; peel and quarter. Add beet plus 1 tsp smoked paprika, cumin, or a combination when combining all ingredients. Reduce tahini to 2 Tbs or omit if desired; same goes for the olive oil.

Spiced Carrot

Rough chop 3–4 peeled or well-scrubbed carrots (up to 1 lb), toss with 1–2 Tbs olive oil and sprinkle with salt and pepper, and roast on a rimmed baking sheet at 425° until tender and lightly browned, about 25 minutes, stirring once or twice. When combining ingredients, add roasted carrots plus up to 3 tsp total of your choice of spices;

cinnamon, ginger, cloves, cumin, allspice, cardamom, coriander, smoked paprika, nutmeg, mace, turmeric, and cayenne pepper are all good choices. The more the merrier, but I recommend no more than ½ tsp of any one spice, and no more than ¼ tsp of the more potent ones such as cloves and cayenne. Use water or bean liquid instead of additional olive oil, if desired.

Brownie Batter

Cut the lemon juice to 1 Tbs and eliminate garlic, pepper, and olive oil. Do not add any salt until you taste test. Add ¼ cup cocoa powder, ½ tsp vanilla, and 1–3 Tbs liquid sweetener such as maple syrup, agave, or honey (start with 1 Tbs). Replace the tahini with creamy peanut butter or another nut butter if desired. Thin with water, bean liquid, or coconut milk. A sprinkle of cinnamon and a tiny dash of cayenne take this to a whole new level, and stirring in a handful of mini chocolate chips at the end sends this into the party zone.

> Note: no food processor or blender? No problem. Hummus has been around a lot longer than electric appliances. Mash it! It won't be smooth, of course, but it'll taste delicious. Just make sure you finely mince your garlic cloves before tossing them in.

A Shift in Perspective

OLIVIA PEITSCH

. . . .

Set your minds on things that are above, not on things that are on earth.
Colossians 3:2 ESV

I stared at my blue-tinted fingers as my husband tried to comfort me. "This is the ugliest cake I've ever made," I moaned. After a morning of guiding small hands as they tried to measure out ingredients and constantly reminding that we turn our heads away from food when we cough, I was excited to assemble a special cake for my son's fourth birthday party the next day. I had successfully removed the cakes from the pans and trimmed them to a smooth, level surface. All that was left was the decorating.

I should have learned this about myself by now, but my cake decorating skills are . . . lacking. I have grand visions in my mind that I can never quite execute in real life. I had a plan for simple piping when my husband reminded me that a *Paw Patrol* cake was requested. Of course.

After I'd mixed up some questionable colors and had several piping bags burst open, the cake was a sight to behold. It wasn't just disappointment I felt; it was frustration, embarrassment, and absolute rage. Not only did I make the world's ugliest cake but I also had to put it on display for guests at a birthday party. And to top it off, nothing about it even hinted at *Paw Patrol*.

I hid the cake in the pantry and hoped my son didn't remember that I'd told him he could see the finished dessert after his nap, but, of course, toddlers have a special space in their brains for the things we hope they forget. As I unveiled the horror that was this cake, my son's eyes lit up. "Is that my cake?" he asked in a reverent tone.

"Yes . . . ?" I responded hesitatingly.

"I love it so much. Thank you, Momma!"

What? Do you need your eyes checked, kid? This cake is a monstrosity.

My son went off to color, and I looked at my husband, who was unsuccessfully trying to hide a smirk. "I told you he would still love it," he said.

I glared and responded under my breath, "It's still ugly."

"It doesn't matter. He wanted a cake made by his mom, and that's what he got."

When the anticipated party commenced, and I cut into the cake and started serving it, something strange happened. The atrocious frosting became the smallest part of the cake. When it was sliced and laid onto plates, what became evident was the perfectly even layer of frosting in the middle and the fluffy chocolate sponge. What was even more surprising was how people dug in, not caring about how it looked. I even received quite a few compliments on the taste.

When our perspectives are not aligned correctly, we can see insignificant things as bigger issues than they are. This cake mishap had the potential to ruin my attitude and taint my memories of an otherwise happy and cheerful celebration. At the end of the day, the cake was gone (Pinterest-worthy or not). The moment had passed, and people still came and left the party. What mattered was the way my son felt celebrated, the friends and family we got to spend extra time with, and the reminder that all of this is possible because of God's great love and grace.

Setbacks are inevitable. In a world tainted with sin, things rarely go how we expect or desire, but how we respond and where we root our hope can make all the difference.

Where have you been focusing your attention lately? Is there something getting in the way of what really matters?

Food from My Storehouse

DARCY SCHOCK

. . . .

For if there is first a willing mind, it is accepted according to what one has, and not according to what he does not have.

2 Corinthians 8:12 NKJV

The burned smell wafted in from the kitchen, greeting me in my hiding place.

Hot on its trail were memories of all my cooking failures, like the strawberry pie that didn't set up in time for a church potluck. Its sticky sweetness dripped over my fingers as I walked it to the table of perfectly baked pies. Or the hour I spent scraping burned noodles off the pan after the last time I hosted a group of friends.

I sniffled and dared a glance at my watch. I had ten minutes to finish cutting the onions for the three soups currently in progress. Ten minutes to swipe away the defeat clouding my mind and smile for my guests.

In a church family that highly values hospitality and cooking, I couldn't figure out what was wrong with me. Why had God missed blessing me with extravagant culinary skills? I knew the value of gathering together around food as a community. But for the life of me, cooking and I weren't getting along.

As I dusted myself off and trailed back to the kitchen, I realized I had been trying too hard to measure up to the hosts surrounding me. No matter how much I tried, my efforts wouldn't bring five-star meals. The lie that I needed to dazzle people with beautiful meals in order to gather friends with success was keeping me stuck and frustrated.

In today's verse, Paul reminds us to give according to what we have, not what we don't. Isn't that such a freeing concept? I had been trying to develop culinary skills I didn't possess. For a time, this kept me from hosting and bringing food anywhere. But I missed the relationships built around the table.

Determined to try again, with the motivation to give what I had, I brainstormed with the best cook I know. She shared with me an easy but mouthwatering recipe for wild rice chicken soup. She assured me I didn't need to cook five-star meals to be worthy of gathering people around my food.

In winter, I make this soup on repeat when I host. It's one that won't stress me out but is delicious. In summer, I usually enlist my husband to grill something while I prepare side dishes I know I can complete with joy and success. In this process, I've realized my friends don't care about my talents as a chef. The heart of gathering around food isn't in my abilities alone but in enjoying savory nourishment together.

God has opened my eyes to the strengths he has given me. I may not create fantastic meals for people, but I am a safe place for hungry souls. When we take pressure off ourselves to give something we don't possess, we gain permission to pour out from the abundance already in us.

Gathering around food is a beautiful thing we all can initiate. Some of us have the gift of cooking gourmet meals that make guests feel incredibly loved. But even if we don't have that culinary skill, we can still bless people with food and do it with joy. As you courageously step into preparing a meal for your next get-together, from the storehouse of your abilities, thank God that he has given us all unique ways to nourish bodies and souls around the wonder of food.

WILD RICE CHICKEN SOUP

Serves 8

2 boxes Ben's Original Long Grain and Wild Rice, Original Recipe
24 oz cream cheese, softened and cubed

2 (10.5 oz) cans cream of chicken soup
2–4 (12.5 oz) cans chunk chicken breast
10 cups water

1. Place everything in a crockpot and heat on low all day, stirring occasionally.

Cereal for Dinner

HELEN ARNOLD

. . . .

*Then the L*ORD *said to Moses, "I will rain down bread from heaven for you. The people are to go out each day and gather enough for that day."*

Exodus 16:4

On occasion, when my kids were younger, I was known to declare, "Cereal for dinner!" My kids would then giggle in delight, run to the pantry, grab bowls from the cupboard, and proceed to pour themselves huge servings of Cheerios.

On the way to the table, they'd drench their cereal with way too much milk and grab a spoon. And then they'd chat happily about their day as they munched their way through at least two bowls.

Our girls loved these days, and even now they'll ask for a cereal dinner as a treat. But what they seem blissfully unaware of is that those cereal days were because of my exhaustion following a day of school runs, kids bickering, and an overwhelming patient load in the clinic where I worked.

After the kids were in bed, guilt had a habit of needling its way into my tired soul. *Your kids needed a better meal than that.... YOU needed a better meal than that.... This was the third day in a row of cereal dinner. What happened to your planned cottage pie, spaghetti, and tacos?*

I remember on one occasion, after a particularly rough day at work and parenting alone when my husband was out of town, we'd had cereal for dinner for four days straight. After my girls were in bed and a load of laundry was in the washing machine, I flopped on my bed and asked God for energy to do tomorrow well.

As I sat there, I opened my Bible and found myself reading this verse: "Then the LORD said to Moses, 'I will rain down bread from heaven for you'" (Exod. 16:4).

In that moment, I recalled that the Israelites ate manna every day for forty years! It was as if God was saying to me, *It's okay. If I can feed the entire Israelite population with the same meal for forty years, four days of cereal for dinner isn't going to harm you or your kids.*

I can't even begin to imagine what it must have been like to eat manna *every day* for forty years! Yet God provided what the Israelites needed in that time, and he provided a pantry full of cereal for those days when I've been working, parenting, and loving my family.

Those cereal dinners, occurring during my most overwhelmed and exhausted days, became some of my family's favorite dinner memories. My girls didn't see my exhaustion or mental overload. They saw an opportunity for a treat, and they saw me loving them and giving them something special.

Sometimes I wonder if this mirrors my relationship with Jesus. It's too easy to forget about the pain Jesus bore on the cross for me. Yet I gladly accept the gifts of love that result—freedom, forgiveness, and acceptance.

Like my kids enjoy their favorite dinner, I enjoy the relationship I have with my Father in heaven because of what Jesus has done. Does Jesus get cross or angry that I don't realize what it cost him? No. We can never fully comprehend what Jesus had to go through for us to have a relationship with him.

Likewise, my girls will never fully comprehend that those cereal dinners came from me being in a hard place. I will never tell them how exhausted and overwhelmed I was in those moments, because like Jesus delights in us being with him, I delighted in my kids' joy, even if it came from a place of personal cost.

Can you think of a time when God took your struggles and turned them into a meal of joy? Or when he's rained bread from heaven to sustain you in your day?

NOT SO SECRET GRANOLA

Serves 5 generously

3 cups old-fashioned oats
⅔ cup chopped, unroasted, unsalted
   almonds
⅓ cup chopped pecans
½ tsp allspice
½ tsp salt

½ cup melted coconut oil
½ cup maple syrup
1 tsp vanilla extract
chopped-up banana and a handful of
   chocolate chips (optional)

1. Preheat oven to 350°.

2. Line a large rimmed baking sheet with parchment paper.

3. Combine all ingredients in a large mixing bowl. Mix well, until evenly coated.

4. Pour mixture onto baking sheet and spread into an even layer.

5. Bake for 20–25 minutes, until golden brown, stirring about halfway through. If you like your granola as clusters, press the mixture down after stirring.

6. Leave to cool completely on the baking sheet. The granola will crisp up as it cools.

7. Once cool, break granola into smaller pieces and transfer to an airtight container. It's best eaten within 2 weeks. (Or store in a sealed freezer bag for up to 3 months.)

8. Serve with milk and top with chopped banana and a sprinkle of chocolate chips, if desired.

Cravings

KATELYN VAN KOOTEN

. . . .

Many nations will come and say, "Come, let us go up to the mountain of the Lord, *to the temple of the God of Jacob. He will teach us his ways, so that we may walk in his paths." . . . Everyone will sit under their own vine and under their own fig tree, and no one will make them afraid, for the* Lord *Almighty has spoken.*

Micah 4:2, 4

While the rest of the family would crowd around for servings of my grandparents' Sunday dinner, ten-year-old me would double back to the kitchen to make myself a peanut butter sandwich. I'm not so picky now that I'm an adult, but there are a few things I refuse to eat—so I can sympathize with the Israelites in Numbers 11. In this story, the people are somewhere between their miraculous exodus from Egypt and their arrival at the land that, hundreds of years earlier, God had promised to give to his people. The book of Exodus recounts the wondrous ways God had provided for this generation so far: inflicting plagues on their enslavers, guiding them as pillars of fire and cloud, and providing a mysterious substance called manna to sustain them.

Still, some of the people got fed up with eating manna every day. Here's what "the rabble [with] greedy cravings" started saying: "Who will give us meat to eat? We remember the fish which we used to eat for free in Egypt, the cucumbers, the melons, the leeks, the onions, and the garlic; but now our appetite is gone. There is nothing at all to look at except this manna!" (Num. 11:4–6 NASB).

I understand missing the pleasures of eating meat and fresh fruits and veggies—I would have been desperate for some garlic and onions, myself—but there's something odd here. Even if this Egyptian food had really been given to them "for free," there had still been an incredible cost! Did they not remember the slavery and oppression, the forced labor, the beatings, the murders of their newborn sons?

And this isn't the only time the Israelites seem to romanticize their time under Pharaoh's tyranny. Throughout Exodus and Numbers, when things start to get difficult, the people reminisce about life in Egypt—and even seriously consider turning back a couple times! Remember, the Israelites were on their way to the promised land, the abundant place "flowing with milk and honey" (Exod. 3:8). They just weren't there yet, and they doubted God's promise was worth this uncomfortable slog through the desert.

My walk with the Lord can sometimes feel like a long trek through an unappealing wilderness. Like the Israelites, I have seen the work of God in my life—the rescuing, the faithful guidance, the provision. Yet I sometimes look back at the things he has freed me from and wonder if it wouldn't hurt to backtrack, even just for a little while. I focus on the memory of temporary pleasures rather than the true cost of sin in my life.

Hundreds of years after their time in the wilderness, the prophet Micah would tell these Israelites' descendants of a future when people will flock to the temple of God to learn his ways, a time of flourishing and peace under the rule of the anti-Pharaoh, our good and wise Lord (Mic. 4). Micah describes the people resting beneath fruit trees and vines that will be *their own*, bearing fruits they won't have to trade their freedom for.

This future—a promise for us too—will be even better than the Israelites' promised land, a harmonious merging of heaven and earth. This is the future destination God had in mind when he first called us out of our life-stealing captivity to sin.

When the Israelites grew tired of their manna-fueled passage through the desert, they had a choice: they could forfeit their freedom for the temporary thrill of some fish and leeks, or they could decide that even though they didn't have everything they wanted in that moment, they could trust God to be true to his word and bring them into a land that was so much better than the one they'd left behind.

So when we feel the "greedy cravings" in our hearts for the savor of sin, remember that sweeter things are coming. Trust that God has something better for us than the things our appetites hunger for. And keep journeying with him.

A Little Learning Goes a Long Way

EMILY UEBBING

· · · ·

We rejoice in our sufferings, knowing that suffering produces endurance, and endurance produces character, and character produces hope, and hope does not put us to shame, because God's love has been poured into our hearts through the Holy Spirit who has been given to us.

Romans 5:3–5 ESV

I did not start out as an adult who knew how to cook. I liked cooking, but I was limited to the small number of things I knew how to make. I would follow a recipe exactly as it was written, never straying from the instructions. I was not confident enough to try adding or substituting ingredients here or there.

Then two different experiences with food changed my view of cooking. The first occurred when my husband and I had returned from visiting my grandmother. We arrived home in the early evening. Since she had taken us out to lunch, we were not keen on eating out again. In one of those infamous moments, after I declared we had nothing to eat, my husband opened the freezer and cabinets, looked at what we had, and told me to relax. The next thing I knew we were eating beef burgundy. No, it was not the twenty-seven-step recipe, and it didn't take hours to cook. But it was one of the most delicious things I had ever tasted, and I was impressed.

The second experience occurred a few months later when we decided to try making a pesto dish. I was feeling more confident, having watched some cooking shows. What could be so difficult about pesto? We made it together and had gotten about halfway through eating our pasta with fresh pesto when we learned there is such a thing as too much garlic. And then I read how many servings this recipe made: eight. The two of us were eating three times as much garlic as the recipe called for in each serving. All we could do was laugh. I don't remember how long it took for our breath to recover, but it's a memory we still chuckle about.

After those two experiences, I felt like I could do this cooking thing. I started watching more cooking shows (as a visual learner living miles from my family, this was helpful) and began trying recipes.

I may have started out troubled in the kitchen, but I persevered. Now when I find a recipe, I think about what's possibly missing (does it need an onion or less garlic?). Is there something in it that I don't like? Am I willing to try it, or can I substitute something else? I love to share recipes and my honed skills with others.

I have learned to trust my gut and use the flavors or ingredients I like best. For instance, the recipe below calls for goat cheese, but you could easily use blue cheese or any other kind of soft cheese, if goat cheese is not your favorite. The same goes for the apple. I happen to love the crunch and sour flavor that a Granny Smith gives this dish. You might find you prefer the more subtle flavor of a Jonagold. Whether you follow the recipe exactly or experiment until you find the best combination, don't give up trying new recipes. (And remember to double-check the amount of garlic in your pesto!)

KALE AND FARRO SALAD

This recipe is modified from a Giada De Laurentiis recipe.[*]

Serves 4–6

½ cup walnuts
6–7 Tbs extra-virgin olive oil, divided
½ red onion, diced
1 cup farro, rinsed
2 cups water
2 sprigs fresh oregano (or a couple shakes of dried)

sea salt, to taste
1 lemon
1 orange
1 bunch kale
1 apple (such as Granny Smith or Jazz)
4 oz goat cheese, crumbled

1. Place the walnuts in a small skillet over low heat. Cook, stirring frequently, until lightly toasted, 8–10 minutes. Cool completely and then chop.

2. Heat a large saucepan over medium-high heat. Add 1–2 Tbs olive oil and onion and cook, stirring often, until onion is translucent, about 10 minutes. Add farro and toast, stirring often, for about 4 minutes. Add water, oregano, and salt. Bring to a simmer and cook, stirring occasionally, for 25 minutes or until farro is tender. If you used sprigs of oregano, remove them.

3. Meanwhile, juice the lemon and orange into a large mixing bowl. Add 5 Tbs olive oil and whisk to combine. Dice the apple and add to the bowl. Massage the kale as you remove the leafy part from the stems. Tear or cut leaves into pieces, and add directly to the bowl. Add the hot, cooked farro mixture and allow the heat to soften the kale. Toss to combine. Add goat cheese and toasted walnuts. Serve and enjoy!

* Giada De Laurentiis, "Farro and Kale Salad," Food Network, accessed January 2, 2024, https://www.foodnetwork.com/recipes/giada-de-laurentiis/farro-and-kale-salad-2677285.

The Perfect Ingredient

LEKEISHA MALDON

. . . .

And we know [with great confidence] that God [who is deeply concerned about us] causes all things to work together [as a plan] for good for those who love God, to those who are called according to His plan and purpose.

Romans 8:28 AMP

It was the perfect day as my friends and I prepared for a relaxing outing at Chincoteague Island during our summer beach trip. While we were getting ready, our morning conversation led to a discussion about one of my favorite treats: chocolate chip cookies. One of my dear companions, who happens to be an avid baker, shared that she had experimented with a new ingredient in her most recent batch of cookies. Despite her initial doubts, she was pleasantly surprised to find that this batch turned out to be one of her best yet. The ingredient she didn't think she needed was the perfect addition.

The moment she said that, my mind recalled one of my favorite verses:

And we know [with great confidence] that God [who is deeply concerned about us] causes all things to work together [as a plan] for good for those who love God, to those who are called according to His plan and purpose. (Rom. 8:28 AMP)

Perhaps you ask yourself the same thing I do when reading this verse: *All things?*

Upon further examination of the biblical context, the word translated "all" encompasses a wide range of meanings, including "each," "every," "any," "the whole," "everyone," and "everything."

Even the things that break my heart?

The days I'd rather not sign up for?

The moment when it felt like the carpet had been pulled straight from under my feet?

That's right, my friend—all things.

Like the ingredient in my friend's cookie recipe, God collectively uses every detail of our lives—past, present, and future—to shape something beautiful, including the things we don't think we need.

And verse 29 further explains to us why—so that we can "be conformed to the image of His Son" (AMP).

It is truly remarkable how God reveals his intricate plan to us through those unexpected and sometimes challenging moments we each will face, reaffirming his absolute control over all things. He knows the "ingredients" each of us needs to add to our lives so that we might reflect his character and display his glory to those around us.

We can find comfort in knowing that no experience in our lives is without its purpose, as God possesses the ability to transform it into something valuable. When faced with difficulties, we can remain steadfast in our belief that even in the most arduous of circumstances, our good Father is constantly working behind the scenes and will ultimately bring about good in the fullness of time.

The disappointment we experienced after we were passed up for the promotion.

The strained friendship we thought was solid.

The health report we weren't expecting from the doctor.

The loss of a relationship we didn't see coming.

Or even our own choices we've made that we wish we hadn't.

He uses it all.

And while it might not be the ingredient we would have added, it's worth considering that it is the very thing needed to perfect the recipe of God's purpose for our lives. The essential piece that allows us to become more like Jesus.

Be encouraged that every detail of our lives is placed in the ultimate Baker's hand, and trust that the final product will turn out better than anything we ever imagined.

People Over Pretties

JILL NOBLE

. . . .

Do not lay up for yourselves treasures on earth, where moth and rust destroy and where thieves break in and steal, but lay up for yourselves treasures in heaven. . . . For where your treasure is, there your heart will be also.

Matthew 6:19–21 ESV

I was big enough to know better but little enough that I needed a chair to reach the counter to commit my crime. All of us kids knew where Mom hid the treats. She stashed them in the corner "do not open" cupboard.

One fateful day when a biscuit from the cookie jar did not satisfy, I stealthily slid a chair toward the corner cabinet, then precariously balanced one foot on the chair and one foot in the corner of the counter and slowly opened the cabinet door.

I didn't see Grandma's bone china dishes, which primarily occupied this cupboard. I only had eyes for the bag of candy. I reached in. In one swift motion, as I pulled the bag toward me, I drew Grandma's sugar bowl out with it. I barely saw the precious bowl fall, but the noise it made when it hit the yellow countertop was deafening to my five-year-old ears.

I was disciplined for sneaking the candy, but I don't remember getting into trouble over what I was most apprehensive about: the broken dish. Mom said it was an accident. The last time I saw that bowl, it was in multiple pieces.

Even with young children, I delighted in setting a pretty table. I often used cloth napkins, primarily used "real" dishes, and enjoyed lighting vanilla scented candles to welcome my people to the table.

While I was shopping one day, my eyes fell upon some yellow dinner plates with ornate scalloped edging that sang my name from their place on the shelf. They were relatively inexpensive; I knew in an instant that they belonged on our table. Impulsively, I bought six dinner plates and six lunch plates and floated home to set our dinner table.

Because of their low price feature, I suppose I should have anticipated what was coming. While loading the plates in the dishwasher one evening after dinner, one of my precious littles scarcely bumped the decorative edge of one of the plates—and a yellow chunk broke off. In a flash, I remembered that china sugar bowl and my mom's gentle response. "It's okay," I assured him, squatting down to look into his eyes. "You are worth more to me than that plate." With all my heart, I meant that . . . but I really liked those plates.

As the weeks passed, more and more of those dishes got chips and flecks knocked off the edges. A war raged inside me over trying to keep these plates in good condition and still use them lavishly to love my people.

I learned that praying over plates is holy ground. And I knew before I said "Amen" what I needed to do. With my little people looking on, I boxed up all twelve chipped and not-yet-chipped plates alike and carried them outside, setting them next to the garbage can. My mom had demonstrated "people over pretties" without fanfare over an heirloom bowl. I wanted to live the same way.

One of the few things I asked for after Mom passed was that English bone china set she'd received from her own mother. Growing up, we'd never used Grandma's china. Now, I wanted to use it with my family. Carefully unwrapping the pieces, I was stunned by their beauty. Joy washed over me like a child on Christmas morning as my table filled with lovely china. And as soon as I saw the top of the sugar bowl, I remembered that awful day straddling the counter and the chair when I broke it forty-five years before.

Tears started falling as my gaze and awareness collided. Mom had meticulously glued it back together, resulting in an obviously once-broken, now slightly deformed bone china sugar bowl. That glued-together piece is now one of my most precious physical possessions, reminding me of my priority of loving people over things and where my truest treasure lies.

MOIST AND FRUITY TEA LOAF

From my favorite Brit, Jane Grant Abban, who said in her delightful accent when she served it to me, "Because you can never have enough tea!"

Yields 1 loaf

¾ cup sultanas
¾ cup raisins
1¼ cups freshly brewed tea
 (using 2 tea bags)
2 cups + 1 Tbs all-purpose flour

2 tsp baking powder
1 cup + 2 Tbs brown sugar
1 tsp mixed spice
2 Tbs butter, melted
2 lg eggs, whisked

1. Place sultanas and raisins in a bowl and pour over the hot tea. Cover and allow to soak overnight.

2. Preheat oven to 325°.

3. Line a 2 lb loaf tin with parchment paper.

4. Combine flour, baking powder, brown sugar, and spice in a large bowl.

5. Mix in the melted butter and whisked eggs.

6. Add the sultanas, raisins, and any extra liquid in the bowl.

7. Stir together until thoroughly combined. It will be very wet.

8. Spoon batter into the prepared tin, and bake for 1–1¼ hours or until a toothpick inserted in center comes out clean, covering with foil if the top is browning too quickly.

9. Cool on a wire rack. Slice and serve warm with salted butter and a nice cup of tea (because you can never have enough tea!).

Finding My Footing in the Kitchen (and in Faith)

KATIE M. REID

· · · ·

When I was a child, I spoke and thought and reasoned as a child. But when I grew up, I put away childish things.

1 Corinthians 13:11 NLT

Growing up in the '80s, my family didn't have cable TV, so we entertained ourselves with our own version of *Star Search* with costumes and fake microphones in the living room, recorded mixtapes of our favorite songs from Casey Kasem's American Top 40, and pretended to host our own cooking show.

When I was a tween, I remember one such "home cooking show" where I used what we had on hand—canned cream of mushroom soup—to make soup. I literally put some of it in a mug and called it good. Maybe I added a bit of pepper and some milk too. It was thick, gooey, and gross. Then, to go with it, I made cream of mushroom chicken. I felt so proud of my themed dinner, but I quickly realized I had missed the mark as my family tried politely to eat it.

Fast-forward to my second year of marriage, and I was determined to make something from my fancy Martha Stewart cookbook. I didn't know what most of the ingredients were in the recipes. However, I found one called chicken tonnato for which I had some of the ingredients and some things that were *sort of* similar.

You can imagine my husband's surprise when he graciously tried my concoction, made with love and a lot of culinary missteps. I had the chicken and tuna the recipe called for, but instead of mayo for the sauce I used ranch dressing, instead of lemon juice I used orange juice, instead of capers I used lettuce (big difference!), and instead of white wine I used an equal amount of rum. It was disgusting. We ended up throwing out my hard work and eating frozen pizza.

After decades of practice, I'm now a good cook, known for my cheesy potatoes, chicken shawarma, and jam-packed salads. I still like to get creative in the kitchen, but time and experience have taught me what flavors work together and when it's safe to deviate from the recipe and when it's not. (Yes, never substitute rum for white wine!)

My culinary journey reminds me of our faith walk as Christians. When we first start out, we make a lot of mistakes as we discover what works and what doesn't. But over time and through experience, we discover things that shouldn't be compromised and areas where there is grace and room to approach things differently from someone else while remaining true to God's Word. Just like we don't reprimand a toddler learning to walk for not doing it perfectly, God teaches us along the way as we stick closely to him and learn from him. Our missteps are opportunities to learn from as we get better at following the One who is with us through it all.

Whether or not you find your footing in the kitchen, Jesus loves you every step of the way on this faith journey, and he invites you to grow up in him and his ways as you follow his clear and caring instructions for you in the Bible.

Now, what'll it be? Cream of mushroom soup, chicken tonnato, or this jam-packed and delicious Greek salad?

I'd stick with the salad.

COLORFUL GREEK SALAD

Serves 2–4

2 romaine lettuce hearts
1 med cucumber, diced
½ (15 oz) can sliced beets, drained
 (chopped smaller if preferred)
½ cup cherry tomatoes
½ (15 oz) can garbanzo beans, drained

½ cup whole or diced black olives
¼ cup feta cheese
1 Tbs finely chopped fresh mint or basil
⅛ cup sliced yellow banana peppers or
 red onions (optional)
Greek dressing to taste (optional)

1. Cut up romaine hearts, then rinse and pat the lettuce dry or use a salad spinner. Transfer to a large bowl.

2. Add all other ingredients and gently toss.

3. If you'd like, add a Greek dressing and toss again, or omit the dressing (it's flavorful as is). Serve with a side of hummus and pita chips.

Say Yes to the Soup

KRISTEN STRONG*

. . . .

The Lord your God is in your midst, a mighty one who will save; he will rejoice over you with gladness; he will quiet you by his love; he will exult over you with loud singing.

Zephaniah 3:17 ESV

What started out as an amazing college visit for my husband and me with our son that mid-November ended with me in the kind of pain I hadn't experienced since childbirth. In the third quarter of a football game at Texas A&M, while our son watched the game with other students, I stood up too quickly and immediately lost my balance. Cue me rolling down five stadium rows and only stopping when I plowed into an unsuspecting fellow below. Great day, the mind-jarring pain in my elbow, complete with bone protruding under the skin where God never intended, was only outdone by my extreme embarrassment over the entire event.

Thankfully, I had so many jump up to help David and me, including the fellow I landed on like a ton of bricks. As David held my hand, another couple of people helped me walk down what felt like a hundred thousand steps to the nearest aid station. I was then placed in an ambulance and taken to St. Joseph's Hospital in Bryan, Texas, where I had my elbow set and my arm placed in a cast before returning to our hotel room.

Let me confess something to you here: I can be a prideful gal who detests asking others for help. As in, *I hate it.* I shun the idea of being dependent on

* Adapted from Kristen Strong, *When Change Finds You: 31 Assurances to Settle Your Heart When Life Stirs You Up* (Grand Rapids: Baker Books, 2021), 169–72.

others. But a change that bends or breaks you, literally or figuratively, shows you in black-and-white contrast your very real limitations. So here I was, hammered into the humblest of states where I realized what I needed was the one thing I hated needing: help.

No, not help. HELP.

This is what I started to feel the next day as we flew back to Denver. The holiday season had just gained altitude in earnest, and here I was grounded for the foreseeable future. All the problems stood at attention.

I've barely done any shopping. Will I get it all done by Christmas?

We're hosting Thanksgiving. How can I cook such a big meal—not to mention our everyday meals—with a bum arm?

My husband's work schedule has little flexibility. How do I pick my daughter up from school and get her to her myriad of activities when I can't drive?

After landing in Denver and making the drive south toward home, we pulled into our driveway plumb exhausted. When we hauled our tired selves into the front door, I found myself overwhelmed with the most delicious scent I'd ever met in my whole life: bacon potato soup simmering in a slow cooker.

The moment I saw the hardworking slow cooker sitting on our countertop, I started crying. Here, without me having to lift a finger, was provision. Here, without one ounce of my doing, was Love coming down in the form of my friend Aimée, who urged me to sit my hind end down and let the creamy, bacon-y goodness warm me from the inside out.

I took it as the nudge I needed to reach out further for help.

So that's what I did. I asked my small group if we could have meals delivered. And when acquaintances, not even close friends, asked us if they could bring over a meal, I said yes instead of my knee-jerk no. I asked my visiting mother-in-law to join my husband in cooking the majority of Thanksgiving dinner. I asked my friend Allison to help me decorate for Christmas. I asked Aimée if she could pick my daughter up from school when David and the boys' schedules ran off the rails. All the help received brought Philippians 4:19 into clear view: "My God will liberally supply (fill until full) your every need according to His riches in glory in Christ Jesus" (AMP).

God is liberal with his care and blessings—he will fill you to the brim with everything you need, but he may ask you to settle yourself in a more humbling position first.

He may ask you to ask for help.

This change left me plumb worn out from my elbow and ego that constantly throbbed. But in the pain came the learning that it was more than okay—it was actually right—to lean on other people. It was an opportunity dropped from heaven to see people offer their best when I was at my worst. This change stripped so many nonessentials from my life—namely a measure of my pride and so-called self-sufficiency—so I could see the essentials with greater clarity.

I'm not sure what measure of pride your change stripped away, but as you abide in the "new now" in front of you, heed the words of author Anjuli Paschall, detailing a time when she came face-to-face with her own limitations.

> When I got home, I asked for help, begged for it. Instead of pretending, I prayed. It was a slow change—riddled with highs and lows. But here's the thing, love came to me. He came. He met me. And God will find you. Even in your fortress high fear or unbearable shame or tar-like blackness. He will come.[**]

He will come.

He will help you abide through this change—depend on it.

** Anjuli Paschall (@AnjuliPaschall), Instagram caption, February 27, 2020, https://www.instagram.com/p/B9GAYqCpHor/.

When a Recipe (and Life) Breaks Down

OLIVIA PEITSCH

· · · ·

For God alone, O my soul, wait in silence, for my hope is from him.
Psalm 62:5 ESV

Confession time: I am an incredibly impatient baker. I want things to go perfectly the first go, and I don't want to have to wait for things to set. I once frosted a cake before it was completely cooled and ended up with raspberry flavored butter dripping all over my refrigerator in a failed attempt to salvage it.

A recent test in my baking patience was making my great-grandmother's toffee recipe. I'll admit, toffee had never been on my radar as a treat I enjoyed—until I received a package as a gift, and my perspective was forever changed by this melt-in-your-mouth, buttery, chocolatey goodness.

I like to consider myself fairly capable in the kitchen, so I attempted to make my own. I scoped out several tips and tricks online and began to cook the mixture. Everything was going well, and I achieved the "paper bag" coloring that every blog had said to look for. And then it was time to add the vanilla, and I questioned every decision I'd made up to that point. The butter separated, and my beautiful, bubbly mixture became an oily mess.

I'll admit, I do not handle setbacks in the kitchen (or in general) well. Panic ensued as I frantically tried to mix my toffee back into submission. Eventually, after some choice words and frantic googling, my mixture came back together and the toffee was saved.

I've faced similar situations in my own life, and I'm sure you have too. Our perfectly curated plans meet an unexpected disruption. A car breaks down. Our *bodies* break down. Lack of money. Lack of friends. Betrayal. Loss. Heartache. What do we do when the life we expected looks nothing like the life we are given?

I have always been intrigued by the story of Joseph. It's easy to focus on the redemption part of his story, where the anticipated confrontation with his brothers and long-awaited reunion with his father occur, but in the middle there is a surplus of disappointment and waiting. Not only was Joseph sold into slavery by his jealous brothers (who—let's not forget—initially wanted to kill him) but he was wrongfully imprisoned, had hopes of being released, was forgotten about, and eventually remembered two years later when the pharaoh required someone to translate his dreams.

Just like my disastrously separated toffee mixture, things often can look the worst right before they come back together. That phase may be a moment, a season, or even a lifetime. We are not promised an easy life. In fact, the Bible tells us as Christians we will face hardships (John 16:33), but we are promised a reunion with the God who has overcome all the adversities we face. Whether our resolution is found in our earthly lives or in the arms of our Savior, we have the hope and confidence things will improve. Our broken messes will be made whole, and the outcome will be better than we ever imagined.

GREAT-GRANDMA REINHOLT'S TOFFEE

Yields 24 pieces

1 cup butter
1 cup water
¼ tsp salt
1 tsp white vinegar
2 Tbs water

½ tsp vanilla
1 cup chopped milk chocolate
1 cup coarsely chopped pecans

1. In a heavy 2 qt saucepan, combine the first five ingredients.

2. Stir over moderate heat until sugar is dissolved and the mixture starts boiling.

3. Cook to 295–300° (hard crack stage), stirring constantly.

4. Remove from heat and stir in vanilla. Immediately pour into a buttered 11×18 pan.

5. Sprinkle chocolate over the top and cover the pan with foil for 5 minutes, allowing the chocolate to melt.

6. Uncover the pan and spread the melted chocolate evenly with a spatula.

7. Sprinkle nuts over the chocolate, and allow to cool until hard.

8. Break into small pieces and enjoy!

Note: if the mixture does separate, add HOT water 1 Tbs at a time until it comes back together.

The Humble Beet

LINDSEY SPOOLSTRA

· · · ·

I have loved you with an everlasting love; I have drawn you with unfailing kindness.

Jeremiah 31:3

Beetroots don't look like much when you pull them out of the ground. Even after they're clean of dirt—or, say, you see them in that bulk produce bin in the grocery store—they're kind of rough. Dark. Vaguely purplish pink, maybe, but not particularly prepossessing. Why would one ever want to bite into a beet? It's not exactly appetizing.

But oh, the brilliant color within. And I'm not even going to talk about the fancy gourmet beets out there, with their various hues and magical candy stripes. No, just the brilliant magenta juiciness of a run-of-the-mill purple beet is enough for me. Raw, roasted, pickled—I dig beets. (Pardon the pun.) I find them beautiful as well as delicious. Sweet and earthy and evidence of God's creativity and sense of humor (see also kohlrabi).

Maybe you're not on Team Beet with me, though. Maybe beets are on your list of alien foodstuffs. I get it—I had minimal beet exposure until well into my thirties. Or maybe you did have early beet exposure, and that is the problem. Did Aunt Lori's pickled beet salad haunt your childhood nightmares?

Or maybe beets are simply intimidating. Too fancy. Too fussy. Too hard to prep and clean up after.

Try the following recipe for Beet Barley Risotto. It is simple. It is exquisite. It is beautiful. It is beets shining at their best, telling you that you've had them all wrong all this time. You've been living a bad beet script, and it's time to drop the page.

What other stereotypes might you be holding on to? What other scripts do you follow without taking the time to figure out just how accurate they are?

No, I'm not talking about kohlrabi. (Yet.)

I'm talking about the messages you tell yourself. How do you describe yourself? Your value? What you can and can't do?

Are you holding a script that says you're a bit rough and unprepossessing—grubby, even, and certainly not enough? *I'm not smart enough to figure it out. I'm not good at being responsible. I'm a terrible leader. I can't handle a situation like this. I don't have enough experience to do that. I can't help it; it's too hard for someone like me to change. I'm a boring person; why would anyone want to be with me?*

Or maybe your script says you're a bit too much—too pungent, too glossy, too . . . apt to stain the tablecloth? *I'm too loud and passionate. I'm too young to be taken seriously. I'm too clumsy to be any good with my hands. I'm always in the way. I've made too many mistakes to ever serve God. I'm too weak to handle that kind of problem. I've always been the silly one, and that's just who I am. My emotions are too much to handle, so I can't share them.*

Are any of these things true? Maybe. Maybe you really are too loud or too quiet for your context. Maybe you do let inertia keep you pinned in an unhealthy place. Maybe you could benefit from learning how to talk through your emotions with a professional counselor. Maybe in your past you were not responsible, or there was an incident when you lacked courage. I don't know. But I do know that is not all of who you are.

Take a good, hard look at that script. Perhaps some of it is true, but not all of it. Perhaps some of it used to be true—and isn't any longer. Ask yourself, *Is this belief accurate? Where does it come from? Would I think it was fair to describe another person like this? Is it from a biased perspective? Is it in line with who the Word of God says I am?*

Now let it go. Your beautiful beets are waiting.

For he chose us in him before the creation of the world to be holy and blameless in his sight. (Eph. 1:4)

BEET BARLEY RISOTTO

Adapted from a Mark Bittman recipe.[*]
Serves 4

1½ cups pearled barley
5–6 cups vegetable stock or water
2 Tbs olive oil
1 med onion, chopped
salt and pepper to taste

1 lb beets, peeled and grated
2–3 packed cups chopped beet greens,
  Swiss chard, spinach, or arugula
½ cup chopped walnuts (optional)
4 oz chèvre (optional)

1. In a large, dry skillet over medium heat, toast barley for 3–5 minutes or until golden and fragrant. Remove from the pan. Meanwhile, place stock or water in a medium saucepan to warm over low heat.

2. After barley has been removed, add olive oil to the skillet. When hot, add onion and cook over medium heat, stirring occasionally, for 3–5 minutes or until softened. If your pan seems dry, add a little more olive oil. Return toasted barley to the pan with the onions, and cook and stir for 2–3 minutes, until barley is glossy and coated with oil.

3. Sprinkle with salt and pepper. Add about ½ cup warm stock, stirring and scraping up any browned bits from the bottom of the pan, until the liquid bubbles away.

4. Ladle in about 1 cup stock, stir, and bring to a gentle boil. When the stock has just about evaporated, add more. Stir after each addition. The mixture should be neither dry nor soupy. You may have to adjust the heat to keep it bubbling gently. Stir frequently.

5. After about 15 minutes, add grated beets. Continue cooking the same way, stirring and adding additional warm stock as it evaporates, until barley is tender, about 15–20 more minutes. You might not use all the stock.

6. When the barley is as tender as you like, add the chopped greens a handful at a time, stirring in each addition until wilted. Taste and adjust the seasoning.

7. Garnish with walnuts and/or dollops of chèvre if desired, and serve hot. (If you prefer to serve room temperature or cold, hold off on adding the cheese.)

Note: if whole-grain (hulled) barley can easily be obtained, it's worth it, though it takes longer to become tender. In step 5, cook an additional 10–15 minutes before adding the beets; be prepared to cook a bit longer than 20 minutes after adding the beets.

[*] Mark Bittman, "Barley Risotto with Beets and Greens," Mark Bittman, accessed November 21, 2023, https://markbittman.com/recipes-1/-risotto-with-beets-and-greens.

A Pop of Connection

MARIA LEONARD

. . . .

My command is this: Love each other as I have loved you.
John 15:12

Love is action; it can be *seen*, and it requires connection. One of the people who has taught me a lot about this is my mother-in-law, Jandra. She has shown me that love doesn't have to be elaborate, expensive, or fancy . . . but it does require being intentional. It is connecting over and over again. Food is a wonderful way to connect with others and show love and support.

Jandra gave us a popcorn popper during our first year of marriage. It was a perfect gift from her because she *loved* popcorn. She loved making popcorn for her family. Every significant gathering included popcorn, and popcorn at the movies was a sure thing. I love that she connected with us by giving the popper. It became part of *our* significant gatherings, both big and small. In fact, twenty-eight years and six children later, I would love to know how much corn popping mileage it has . . . too bad it didn't come with a pop-o-meter!

She also gave us the biggest stainless steel bowl I have ever seen—also for popcorn. I think it came from a feed store, just like hers. When she would visit, Jandra would fill it with popcorn. The huge bowl would stay out on the table, and countless movies, stories, games, and meaningful conversations happened around it. I have memories of little hands reaching in and sweet talks happening all around. This simple, loving act of connecting over popcorn has been anticipated and enjoyed year after year.

When our family moved to Korea, and we were unable to buy the kind of butter needed for one of our children who had serious food allergies, Jandra popped and buttered a ginormous box of popcorn and mailed it to us—more than once! This was love in action and connection over thousands of miles, and it spoke volumes of our little boy's importance; he was *not* going to miss out on popcorn. And when she came to visit, she filled her carry-on suitcase with butter! Airport customs must see it all, but what may have looked like a carry-on full of butter was actually a carry-on full of practical love. This was an act of intercontinental connection!

A sad day came recently when that faithful, battle-worn popcorn popper died. I felt sad as I stood in the kitchen looking at it, willing it to go on. But then I began to think of all the love and support it represented, the connection that came for our family through popcorn and through Jandra's willingness to consistently provide support in big and little ways. She showed us love using something very simple: popcorn. Popcorn makes us feel very close to Jandra.

Jesus shows us love through action and connection in John 21:15–17 when he speaks to Peter following Peter's three betrayals.

> When they had finished eating, Jesus said to Simon Peter, "Simon son of John, do you truly love me more than these?"
>
> "Yes, Lord," he said, "you know that I love you."
>
> Jesus said, "Feed my lambs."
>
> Again Jesus said, "Simon son of John, do you love me?"
>
> He answered, "Yes, Lord, you know that I love you."
>
> Jesus said, "Take care of my sheep."
>
> The third time he said to him, "Simon son of John, do you love me?"
>
> Peter was hurt because Jesus asked him the third time, "Do you love me?"
>
> He said, "Lord, you know all things; you know that I love you."
>
> Jesus said, "Feed my sheep."

Jesus isn't angry at Peter; in fact, he connects with him over a meal. Jesus cares for him by including Peter in conversations about future projects. He shows him love. Jesus also prompts Peter to make his love an action. *Feed. . . . Take care of . . .*

I just ordered a new popper, and it has already been used three times in the three days we've had it. Poor thing doesn't know what it's in for!

As I busy myself with the particulars of life, I've begun asking myself, *How can I do this very practical loving for others? What popcorn-type connectors have I been given that I can use to show love to those around me? How am I feeding his sheep?*

Kneads Improvement

NAOMI ZYLSTRA

. . . .

Do not merely listen to the word, and so deceive yourselves. Do what it says.
James 1:22

I've been a baker since fifth grade, when my mom told me I was old enough to use the oven all by myself. To me, this was a true sense of independence and power. I could have fresh cookies or brownies whenever I wanted them, without having to wait on anyone else's baking whims. When I first started baking, I would make something almost every week—to my family's delight.

I've kept up with the hobby and have recently dipped my toe into bread-making. Making bread has deep biblical roots, and a fresh loaf of bread can bring so much comfort and joy. This is the food vessel that Jesus called his own body. It was the food that fed the Israelites and was the center of several miracles. It is also the same food we use during communion at my church. Plus, I really like eating bread, and I'd noticed the large artisan loaves at the grocery store were getting expensive. With my skill, I thought I could make my own bread easily, right? How difficult could it be?

I quickly realized making bread is a whole different beast than baking chocolate chip cookies. I still feel like I'm only scratching the surface, but I've learned that bread can be much more about *feeling* than simply following a recipe. Yes, absolutely I need a recipe, but elements like temperature, time, and humidity also affect the outcome of the bread.

I've gotten enough basic experience that I can tell if a dough is too wet or—as I unfortunately learned more recently—overproofed. I waited too long during the proofing period, and the outcome was a dense loaf.

My goal, at the end of this learning process, is to make perfect breakfast toast. There's a certain loaf from a local bakery I grew up with that's a cross between an English muffin loaf and a sandwich bread loaf. It's got a crunchy exterior and chewy middle and goes great as toast. Since this bakery won't give away their recipe, I've been experimenting with recipes on my own.

Most of the breads I've made have been good but missing something. As I tried and failed on my first attempt at my own recipe (remember the overproofing?), I reflected on how my attempt compared to the bread in my memory—and how this is similar to Christians who are called to be imitators of Christ.

I could imagine how I wanted the bread to taste and feel. I was familiar with the consistency of the bread from my childhood, but when I tried making it on my own, my attempt was dense and flavorless.

I know who Christ is, and I can ask myself how Jesus would act if he were in my situation, but often my own life doesn't look like Christ's life here on earth. I intend to love my neighbors but end up judging them instead. I don't mean to be prideful but end up relying on myself when I should be looking to God.

My life is an approximation of Christ's and I'm doing my best, but I know I can never be a perfect imitation. But that doesn't mean I'm going to stop trying.

The loaves I make are not exactly the bread I remember in childhood, but I am still making bread and improving my technique and outcome each time I try. I'll never be done tweaking my breadmaking. Each difference in temperature and humidity means the bread dough needs different adjustments, just like life. Each day as an imitator of Christ is going to call for different virtues too. Maybe one day will call for heaps of kindness and patience when my spouse has had a rough day. Or another day a friend may need honesty and integrity from me. Just as I continue to make small changes in my breadmaking, I will continue to pay attention to how the people around me need Christ's love for that day.

Gracias, Guacamole!

MAUREEN MILLER

· · · ·

And Jesus grew in wisdom and stature, and in favor with God and man.

Luke 2:52

N ow *that's* guacamole!"

My husband dipped another chip, then popped it in his mouth.

"Hey, how 'bout some chip with your guac!" I laughed.

"But it's so good, just like José's."

I knew what he meant. Years ago, while dining out in San Antonio, we'd ordered tableside guacamole. As the server parked his cart beside us, I pulled out my notepad. Slicing and dicing—sprinkling salt pinched between fingers—the server created his masterpiece before our eyes, and I scribbled away.

Reading his name tag, I smiled. "Wow, José! That's some good-lookin' guac."

"Gracias."

Finished with his creation, José dipped his head in our direction. "Disfruta la comida!"

Oh, enjoy it we would! Then, in unison, we said, "Gracias, José!"

I think about this encounter every time I prepare guacamole for family and friends—hearing the smack of lips and "Mmm!"

And just as I put pencil to paper so I'd remember the recipe of this Mexican favorite, I think our sweet Savior, too, watched in earnest as Joseph carved wood in the carpentry shop. While Mary kneaded dough for bread, adding a sprinkle of salt pinched between fingers. Taking note—though perhaps not on parchment. I believe Jesus was a student too.

He was human, after all. And while perfect, he learned from those around him, those he loved and who loved him in return. Do you think he fashioned a chair? Learned to prepare food for guests, then serve them?

A poignant Christmas movie, *The Nativity Story*, always brings me to tears, though I've watched it many times. In one scene, Joseph ponders aloud, "Sometimes I wonder if I'll even be able to teach him anything."

But teach him he and Mary would, in subtle though powerful ways—at least depicted in this film.

In another scene, Joseph holds back a portion of his meager supper. After Mary goes to sleep, he gives the small piece of pita to their hungry donkey, demonstrating *sacrifice*, even toward this humble beast of burden. In another, an exhausted Joseph falls asleep, his feet dirty and blistered from days of tedious travel. Mary takes time to *serve* her husband by washing them, despite her own fatigue. Finally, witnessing merchants selling their wares in the temple, Joseph demonstrates *righteous anger*. He recognizes what was hurtful to the heart of God and, thus, it hurts his heart too.

These three actions—sacrifice, service, and righteous anger—imply that Jesus would learn from his parents while he was with them. Being their son, something God orchestrated for a reason, means Jesus looked to his parents as teachers—earthly guides pointing him to what was pleasing to his heavenly Father.

Even more, we know Jesus was a student because Scripture tells us so. Take, for example, the story of an adolescent Jesus staying behind in the temple to sit with religious leaders. When Mary asked why he would treat them this way, he responded, "Didn't you know I had to be in my Father's house" (Luke 2:49)?

There are many examples throughout the New Testament that remind us of Jesus's dependence upon his Father, exemplified when he'd separate from others to be alone in God's presence. As Luke's Gospel says, "But Jesus often withdrew to lonely places and prayed" (5:16).

Indeed, I believe Jesus learned—from his parents, from others, and, most importantly, from his heavenly Father. Perhaps he baked bread in the kitchen with Mary. Likely, he carved wood to create furniture in Joseph's workshop. Undoubtedly, as a youth, Jesus reasoned with religious teachers—yes, learning from them, even if the lesson was what *not* to do! And Jesus certainly learned from his Abba all thirty-three years of his earthly life.

This truth encourages me, reminding me to be a student—to never stop learning, whether memorizing Scripture or tackling a new recipe. Like José. He certainly learned from someone, then shared his knowledge—making him, and us, both student and teacher.

I guess one could say we're a lot like Jesus—the One who learned and then taught. Yes, he *grew* in wisdom and offers us, his students, the same as we walk with him.

And just like that pinch of salt for flavor, we're called to be salt in the world. Gracias, Jesus! Gracias!

TABLESIDE GUACAMOLE

Serves 8–10

4–6 ripe avocados, halved and pitted (set one pit aside)
½ lime or lemon
½ orange
chopped cilantro to taste

½ cup chopped sweet onion
1 med tomato, chopped
salt and pepper to taste
dash garlic powder

1. Using a spoon, scoop out avocado flesh into a large bowl. Mash until few lumps remain.

2. Add a squeeze of fresh lemon or lime juice and a squeeze of fresh orange juice.

3. Add cilantro, onion, and tomato. Then add a dash of salt, pepper, and garlic powder to taste. Mix until well blended.

4. Take reserved avocado pit and tuck down into the guacamole. (Best-kept secret! This will keep the guac from browning, but be sure to tell guests it's there.) Serve with chips. Enjoy!

An Extra Special Ingredient

DARCY SCHOCK

. . . .

If I give away all I have, and if I deliver up my body to be burned, but have not love, I gain nothing. . . . So now faith, hope, and love abide, these three; but the greatest of these is love.

1 Corinthians 13:3, 13 ESV

With a pie knife, I slice together powdery flour and slick Crisco to form a doughy ball. My daughter stands next to me, tiptoes on a white step stool. Her chin barely reaches above the counter. With a determined look on her face, she whisks together the cream, eggs, and sugar from a recipe handed down by my grandmother.

Her small, flour-streaked fingers combining the mixture make it at least four generations of ladies who have used this recipe.

This is no ordinary apple pie. Anytime I make a recipe from my grandmother, I know it holds an extra-special ingredient. One she never voiced, yet God has opened my eyes to its existence and power over the years.

After we pour the apples and filling into the crust, I slide the pie in the oven and turn to wipe off the counter. My mind wanders to my grandmother. She lived so full of joy and spunk. Yet she didn't have an easy go of it.

In a dark season of my life, God opened my eyes to her radiant legacy. How was she so happy? How did her companionship always seem to hug my heart? I had the privilege of tasting a bit of her life, and ever since she left this earth, I've yearned for more of it.

What made her demeanor so sweet? The things we did together were fun, but the way she made me feel lasted so much longer than the acts themselves.

Her presence radiated even brighter than her purpose.

Purpose is a good thing. The tasks we complete are needed and powerful. But from observing Grandma's life, I have found that they aren't the only things, or what is most important. If she accomplished many noble works in her life, but in the process made me feel rushed or shamed, I wouldn't look back on the memories we made together with such fondness.

Grandma's example taught me it's not so much about what we do as how we do it. She was a living reflection of 1 Corinthians 13. She had an extra special ingredient in her life, and my palate sensed it. It was the love in which she did everything.

That is the thing I want most prevalent in my life as well.

The buzzer dings, and I pull out the golden brown pie. Steam rises, and the scent of cinnamon lingers heavily in the air. My daughter is licking her lips in anticipation of melting ice cream piled in a mound atop a warm, gooey slice.

As her eyes light with excitement, my heart warms with gratitude. I am grateful for the legacy my grandma handed down. Thankful that there is more in this pie than just sugar and eggs. I pray that the same love, woven into the very recipe, handed down through generations, will come at just the right moment to teach my daughter profound lessons.

I pray she will sense the sweetness of love in the invisible legacy my grandma left. That she will taste it in the life I am living. Then, in the exact moment God sees fit, she will understand its depth and beauty and how it holds the key to sweetness in her own life. Love's impact is far greater than our eyes can see, and it outlives us, spanning the course of countless generations.

Love is the extra special ingredient in our lives that makes everything we do taste especially good.

APPLE PIE

Serves 6–8

1 unbaked pie crust
2 Tbs + 1 Tbs flour
1 cup + 1 Tbs sugar
4–5 apples, peeled and cut into
  thin slices

1 egg, beaten
1 cup half-and-half
additional brown sugar, butter, and
  cinnamon

1. Preheat oven to 400°.

2. If necessary, arrange dough for crust in pie plate, pressing gently into the bottom and up the sides, and trimming edges and/or crimping as desired. Sprinkle about 1 Tbs flour and 1 Tbs sugar over the bottom of the crust.

3. Place sliced apples in the crust.

4. Mix beaten egg, remaining flour and sugar, and half-and-half in a bowl, then pour over the apples.

5. Sprinkle with brown sugar, a few small slices of butter, and cinnamon to your liking.

6. Bake at 400° for 20 minutes, then turn the oven down to 375° and continue baking for an additional 25 minutes, until golden brown.

The Cross-Cultural Power of Food

ERIN BARTELS

· · · ·

Love the sojourner, therefore, for you were sojourners in the land of Egypt.
Deuteronomy 10:19 ESV

In 2010, a group of Chin Christian refugees from Myanmar called up my church, Judson Memorial Baptist, and let us know that God had led them to us. You see, our church in Michigan's capital city was named after the first missionary from America, Adoniram Judson, who spent forty years in what was then Burma, bringing the gospel to a region considered impossible to evangelize. Nearly two centuries later, the descendants of those first Burmese Christians were knocking on the door of a building emblazoned with his name. Obviously, this was where God wanted them.

And so began my association with Za Uk Lian and his family. Between English lessons, homework help, sorting through mail, and navigating shady landlords, I spent much of my free time for the next seven years at Za's kitchen table. And they usually set out something for me to eat or drink as we worked together.

One day a large bowl holding an entire cut-up cantaloupe appeared before me. I don't particularly like cantaloupe, but I didn't want to be rude. It wasn't until I'd eaten about half the bowl that it occurred to me that perhaps we were all meant to share it.

Whenever I brought my young son with me to their house, he came home with strange Asian candies that tasted like medicine. I was often served Asian energy drinks at four in the afternoon.

One night, Za and his family invited us over for a big dinner. Among the offerings on the table were fried chicken and watermelon—two American staples they had adopted immediately and enthusiastically—as well as typical Chin fare like yellow rice, vegetables, and spicy dried peppers. Oh, and boiled intestines. My husband and I piled our plates with rice, vegetables, chicken, and watermelon, so as to leave no room for intestines. But when I wasn't looking, my helpful host slipped some onto my plate anyway.

Boiled intestines are exactly what they sound like. Nothing more, nothing less. No spices. No sauce. No breading that might mask the texture. In fact, I could clearly make out the little papillae on the inside of the quivering white tubes, meant to "move things along," as it were.

As a texture person, I did not want to eat these. They reminded me of octopus, which I don't like. But as a guest in someone else's house, I had to. I cut a few into very, *very* small pieces to mix in with the rice. Regardless, it was hard to get it down, and I felt a little queasy.

Over the years, I ate a lot of interesting Chin food. Fish heads at weddings. Eye-wateringly spicy soups. And a plastic grocery bag of loose, unpackaged mystery meat that had been sitting on the kitchen counter for at least two hours before it was handed to me as a thank-you gift.

"What kind of meat is this, Za?"

"Cow."

"Beef. But what cut? Like, what part of the cow did this beef come from?"

"It's cow."

I took the room temperature cow meat home and made it into beef stroganoff, and no one got sick.

Eventually, my time with Za and his family came to an end. I had gotten three of them successfully through the citizenship process. I had tried to explain why so many English words were spelled so strangely. I had assisted at doctors' offices and eye appointments. I had helped the boys with their college applications. I had helped keep them from being evicted. I had sat with the family in the hospital as Za died.

And they had taught me how to live entirely by faith. With nothing but the clothes on their backs, they had come as sojourners to a strange, cold land where they couldn't communicate easily, where they lived in substandard housing in dangerous neighborhoods, where many thought of them as a burden on the taxpayer, a drain on the public coffers. And they trusted God to get them through it.

And they had fed me.

They fed *me*.

The Art of Refinement

ROBIN BUPP

. . . .

[Be] confident of this, that he who began a good work in you will carry it on to completion until the day of Christ Jesus.

Philippians 1:6

When your favorite cooking show makes one of your all-time favorite foods (and makes it look easy), you have to try it out, right? Recently, one of my favorite celebrity chefs made caramels, so naturally I attempted to make them. You may already know the outcome: it was not as easy as they made it look! I didn't have the patience required, I burned myself a few times, and my house smelled like scorched sugar for more than a few days.

Caramel recipes employ a standard candy-making technique: boiling a sugar syrup to high-but-specific temperatures. Unlike other candy, caramel is heated well past the normal clear sugar syrup, until the liquid begins to turn brown; that is where all the complex deliciousness comes from. (And if you go a little higher, that's where that scorched sugar smell comes from!)

The process of making caramels reminded me of these verses:

In all this you greatly rejoice, though now for a little while you may have had to suffer grief in all kinds of trials. These have come so that the proven genuineness of your faith—of greater worth than gold, which perishes even though refined by fire—may result in praise, glory and honor when Jesus Christ is revealed. (1 Pet. 1:6–7)

Peter compares the building of our faith to the refining of gold—a process that heats the gold to extremely high temperatures to melt off any impurities and prove its genuineness. Pure gold has been prized as valuable by many societies, both for its rarity and for its inert durability. I have a gold wedding ring, and I wear it everywhere, all the time, trusting its genuineness. Through the trials of the chlorinated pool and bathroom cleaning chemicals, it remains unchanged. It has proven its purity and durability over all the years I've worn it.

As gold must be refined, our far more valuable faith must be refined as well. Trials provide the heat that will prove our faith—not to God, who already knows our hearts, but to us! And trying circumstances will melt away the lesser things we might try to place our faith in. Trials are rough stuff, but they aren't to harm or destroy us—they are opportunities to carefully purify our faith. When we make caramel, we don't want to heat the sugar so hot that it burns and becomes unpalatable; rather, we heat it carefully to develop new and unique flavors that are richer, deeper, and more pleasing than the original ones. So with our faith, we learn to trust God in new ways, to know him more deeply and rely on him more fully through our trials.

Trials don't just refine our faith but bring it to maturity or completeness (see James 1:2–4). Tough times and challenges are not easy or desirable, but I am encouraged that, when I find myself in those times, I can trust God is growing my faith, making it more complete and sound, deepening my trust in him.

CARAMEL BROWNIES

Yields 15 brownies

1 (5 oz) can evaporated milk, divided
½ cup butter, softened (not melted)
1 box German chocolate cake mix

1 cup chocolate chips (plus additional if desired)
14 oz soft caramels

1. Preheat oven to 350°. Prepare an 11×7 baking pan with nonstick spray. (If you don't have an 11×7, the recipe will also fit into an 8×8 AND a 4×8 loaf pan.)

2. Mix together ⅓ cup evaporated milk, softened butter, and cake mix (optional: add ½–¾ cup chocolate chips to this batter).

3. Spread half of the batter into prepared pan and bake for 10 minutes.

4. While that is baking, melt caramels and remaining evaporated milk in a saucepan over low to medium heat, just until caramels are melted and creamy.

5. Remove pan from oven; sprinkle evenly with 1 cup chocolate chips, then evenly pour the melted caramel over the entire base. Top with the rest of the batter. (It is sometimes easiest to break off balls of batter, flatten them with your palms like pancakes, and fit them like puzzle pieces over the caramel layer; it is okay if some caramel spots are showing.)

6. Bake for another 15–20 minutes, until the brownie is set, then remove from the oven and cool before slicing.

The Ministry of Hospitality

A Safe Place to Feast

JENNY ERLINGSSON

. . . .

So in everything, do to others what you would have them do to you.
Matthew 7:12

I don't have to worry about my child here." I looked up at my friend in understanding as she shared these words with me from across my counter. We had invited a couple families over for a Saturday afternoon brunch of sorts. When we lived in the States, we loved hosting groups and families at our home, and that hadn't changed after our move to Iceland. But as I stumbled through a new language, I also had to learn the Icelandic names of ingredients. Preparing foods became a more intentional process because I couldn't go with what seemed familiar. Hosting others at my home had to come out of the overflow of my ability to host my own children well, to feed them foods they would enjoy and not be injured by.

Growing up, a few of my siblings dealt with allergies, but those limitations had never been something I thought too much of. I was the older sister who still enjoyed her peanut butter and jelly sandwiches and just made sure to avoid my brother while doing so. But after the birth of our children, we discovered by unfortunate trial and error that they have varying degrees of allergies. Innocent treats are sometimes hazardous. Snacks a sibling can consume produce hives in another child. Certain foods have to be cooked separately, because it's not so fun having a fish allergy when we live in a country whose main industry is fishing. And many of the natural food options like lentils or almond flour or coconut are also a no-go. A couple of my kids have had to learn self-control the hard way. If they are unsure of the ingredients in a cake or cookie, it's best to leave it alone.

Asking others about the ingredients in the food they've prepared is not always the easiest, but I've made it a part of my rhythm of hospitality. Over the years, as our house has filled with coffee times, afternoon snacks for our kids and their friends, prayer gatherings, and meals with other families, I ask about allergies and preferences with diligence. This is not a burden to me because I know how it feels to wonder if the food my child eats will make them miserable or, worse, hospital bound.

As I learned of friends' allergies or medically induced diets, I realized that making little changes to recipes wasn't difficult. I could set aside small portions of the same food with slightly different ingredients. Sometimes I cook meals with multiple options so everyone has a choice. This isn't about burdensome catering but, as I've heard friends say, about loving care. Intentional preparation is an act of compassionate hospitality that makes my guests feel welcome and nurtured.

My friend shared those words with me that day because there are many things her son can't eat. Like me, she knows what it means to read labels carefully and consider every bite. But at our home, her child has his own specially made muffins and biscuits. Not to make him stand out but to allow him to join in breaking bread with us that would not break him.

For another friend, intentional hospitality has allowed her to share in the tradition of Thanksgiving without regrets. She had eyes full of tears and her own cast-iron skillet of green bean casserole that wouldn't add to her ailment.

Every question I ask before guests arrive cultivates an opportunity for deep connection. Their vulnerability is met and valued through the simple act of preparing food.

It's what I want for my kids, but I didn't realize how much that simple intention would create such an atmosphere of safety for others. That those special side dishes would cause the receivers to feel loved in an intimate way. And that by sowing seeds of intentional, individualized hospitality, I would reap that for my kids as well. Others look out for them with intention and care, creating safe places for them to flourish and dwell.

CUSTOMIZABLE MUFFINS

Adapted from Divas Can Cook.

You can modify this recipe to your dietary needs or to your pantry contents with the variations provided. No sugar? Use maple syrup, for example. Don't let a lack of ingredients or perfect measurements keep you from creating.

Yields 10–14 muffins

½–1 cup sweetener (I usually use ¾ cup sugar or ½ cup maple syrup. Sometimes I split the sugar between brown and white. I've also used maple sugar.)

½ cup cooled melted butter, vegetable oil, or coconut oil (a bit less if you use maple syrup for sweetener)

1 egg or egg substitute

¼ cup Greek yogurt or nondairy yogurt (or cream or just a bit more milk; sour cream works as well)

1 tsp vanilla extract

1½ cups flour (I use fine spelt, but use whatever flour you have and follow the ratios on that flour's packaging.)

1½ tsp baking powder

¼ tsp salt

½ cup buttermilk (or 1 tsp lemon juice plus enough milk or alternate milk to make ½ cup; let sit for a few minutes before using)

mix-ins such as chocolate chips, grated apple, cinnamon/nutmeg, dried cranberries, or nuts

1. Preheat oven to 350°.

2. Set out muffin pans and liners.

3. In a large mixing bowl, combine the sweetener and the melted butter/oil. Add egg, Greek yogurt, and vanilla.

4. In a smaller bowl, mix together flour, salt, and baking powder.

5. Pour a third of the buttermilk into the wet ingredients, mix until combined, then add a third of the flour mixture. Mix for a few seconds. Continue alternating between milk and flour until everything is combined.

6. Now, this is where you get to play. If you have a plain muffin lover, take that batter out first. Fill lined muffin cup(s) two-thirds full. Then split your remaining batter based on what other ingredients you mix in. In one bowl, I fold about half a cup batter in with ⅓ cup grated apple, ½ tsp cinnamon, and a sprinkle of nutmeg. In the remaining batter, I fold in ½ cup chocolate chips.

7. Once those batters are in liners, I may stick a sliver of apple peel on top of each apple muffin and then drop a couple chips on top of each chocolate one. That way no one is confused.

8. Cook for 12–14 minutes, based on your oven type, but the best indication is when a toothpick or knife comes out clean.

9. Once done, let cool in tin for 5 minutes, then transfer to a dish or cooling rack—or into your mouth, if you're a risk-taker. If my kids have been extra polite that day, I may let them sprinkle some powdered sugar on top.

* Monique Kilgore, "Moist & Fluffy Chocolate Chip Muffins," Divas Can Cook, June 7, 2018, https://divascancook.com/chocolate-chip-muffins-recipe/.

Loving the Foreigner

MEGHANN AND RAYCE PATTERSON

· · · ·

Truly I tell you, whatever you did for one of the least of these brothers and sisters of mine, you did for me.

Matthew 25:40

Joy and Andy were our support family while we were studying abroad in Ireland. They had hosted American students in the past, and they were well connected to the church we attended while studying there. Their kids were grown up, so they had the free time to invest in some young adults. We had just started dating at the time, and we were surprised to hear that they were comfortable hosting both of us—having us over for meals at the same time, spending time together, and so on. What we didn't realize was how far they would go to make sure we felt like more than guests. They treated us like family.

Over the months we were in Ireland, they cooked us amazing food like traditional Irish brown bread and beef stew and offered us advice in our fledgling relationship. They invited us over to play with their dogs and to see the newborn lambs. When we were at church, they would regularly stop to talk with us about our travels and studies, often for almost an hour after the service was over. Even when they had family members visiting, they would still have us over and treat us like an extension of their family. In a very short amount of time, we began to see Joy and Andy as close friends and almost as beloved as our own parents.

However, the most heartfelt gift Joy and Andy would give us was still to come. A few years after our travels in Ireland, we were engaged and planning our wedding. We invited Joy and Andy to the United States to celebrate with us, but various circumstances prevented them from attending. You can imagine our surprise when a large package from Ireland showed up as a wedding gift. Inside was a beautiful handmade blanket and a letter from Joy and Andy explaining the gift. In their family, it was tradition to give a blanket as a gift to the newlyweds. To say we were overcome with tears of gratitude would be an understatement.

We recently returned to Ireland to relive some memories, visit old friends, and thank Joy and Andy in person for their gift. It was such a blessing to see them again, and it was like nothing had changed. They still talked and laughed with us over tea after church. And even after several years, they still invited us over for a meal in their home.

Leviticus 19:33–34 says, "When a foreigner resides among you in your land, do not mistreat them. The foreigner residing among you must be treated as your native-born. Love them as yourself, for you were foreigners in Egypt. I am the LORD your God."

Joy and Andy lived out this verse by treating us like their family. They took two students in a foreign land and provided us with a place of safety, pouring into our lives with love and wisdom. The hospitality this couple showed us was a rare gift when we needed it most. When we were married and began our own family, we wanted to create a space where we could reflect the same love and hospitality we were shown.

Who in your life needs love and hospitality shown to them? They don't have to be literal foreigners; there are many people in our communities who feel like outsiders. What can you do to "love them as yourself"? What is a way you've been shown love that you would like to reflect to others?

INSTANT POT IRISH BEEF STEW

Serves 4

2 med potatoes, peeled and diced
1–2 lg carrots, peeled and diced
½ cup diced onion
1½ lbs beef roast, such as chuck
2 tsp salt
1 tsp pepper
2 tsp onion powder
2 tsp oregano or Italian seasoning

1 tsp thyme
2 tsp rosemary
1 Tbs minced garlic
¼ cup tomato paste
4 cups beef broth
2 Tbs soy sauce
1 Tbs brown sugar

1. Place diced potatoes and carrots into the Instant Pot. If you prefer larger chunks of potato, boil them for a few minutes before adding to the Instant Pot. Add diced onion.

2. Cut the beef into small chunks and place on top of the vegetables. If you prefer beef to have a tougher texture, you can brown it for just a few minutes on the stove with some butter and extra garlic before adding to the Instant Pot. If you are short on time, adding the beef straight to the pot is a quick and easy trick.

3. Add all remaining ingredients. Stir to mix everything together, and make sure the spices are well incorporated.

4. Set the pressure to "high" and the timer to 35 minutes. Serve with sweet bread or Irish soda bread with some butter on top.

The Gift of a Hot Meal

ALYSSA ROGGIE ALLEN

· · · ·

Each of you should use whatever gift you have received to serve others, as faithful stewards of God's grace in its various forms. If anyone speaks, they should do so as one who speaks the very words of God. If anyone serves, they should do so with the strength God provides, so that in all things God may be praised through Jesus Christ. To him be the glory and the power for ever and ever. Amen.

1 Peter 4:10–11

I t was dinnertime.

I was exhausted. I was not sure I'd showered that day. My first baby was only weeks old. He probably still had not reached his due date, as he had arrived four weeks early. We were both still figuring out nursing.

On my refrigerator was a printed schedule of meals coming from church friends. Every other day, for two weeks, there was a name alongside the dish for that day: Carol's lasagna, Claire's Cobb salad, Bernie's chicken divan.

That day it said: Tess—pot roast.

She arrived, bearing heaping dishes of pot roast, mashed potatoes, corn, and biscuits.

As my husband and I sat eating the pot roast, I distinctly remember thinking, *I have never tasted anything so delicious. This is the best meal of my life.*

Now, that premature, jaundiced little baby is sixteen years old and much taller than me.

On road trips or during table conversations, sometimes we play question games. Inevitably, someone asks, "What's the best meal you have ever had in your life?"

My answer: Tess's pot roast.

The pot roast was melt-in-your-mouth tender and seasoned to perfection (her secret is cooking it for hours in red wine). The mashed potatoes were creamy, and the corn was dripping in butter. It was, by any measure, a delicious meal made by a talented cook.

But I am convinced it was made exponentially more delicious because of things far beyond her secret ingredients and cooking techniques. Things like how it arrived on my doorstep piping hot and ready to devour. How it soothed my tired body and mind. How it infused much-needed calories into my nursing body. And how it reminded me that I was surrounded by other mothers who had gone before me.

I later became the meal ministry coordinator in that same church. I cannot count the meals I've prepared and delivered to new parents, families going through a difficult time, and people who have recently moved. It's one of my favorite things to do.

Every time, I think of Tess arriving on my porch with that pot roast. What's your pot roast? And who needs your gifts today?

The Simplicity of a Bowl of Soup

JILL V. WOODWARD

. . . .

Offer hospitality to one another without grumbling. Each of you should use whatever gift you have received to serve others, as faithful stewards of God's grace in its various forms.

1 Peter 4:9–10

My mother had many talents, but if I had to pick one that stood out above the others, it would be her way of making people feel welcome in our home.

One of my favorite memories is of a night when, for some reason, one of my brothers, my mother, and I were up a lot later than usual. We were talking in the kitchen when we heard a vehicle in the driveway. We looked outside and saw our friend's service truck. He'd had an emergency call to repair a furnace, and while passing by our house at 1:00 a.m., he saw our light on.

"I saw the light on and wondered if I could get a cup of coffee," he admitted. My mother smiled and put the coffee on.

Once upon a time, there was a small church in a small town just outside of New York City. I don't know the early history of that church, just that it had gotten down to five remaining members, and for some time, those five people gathered to pray and ask God to do something.

God did. He called a pastor to that church, and slowly, God added to their numbers. When I started attending the church, there were probably about thirty people. The pastor would greet any visitors from the pulpit. And just about every week, he would say, "It doesn't matter if all you have is peanut butter and jelly. Bring someone home with you for lunch today." And we did. We shared meals, and we got to know each other. New people came, many professing faith for the first time.

Soon there were more than a hundred people, most new to walking with Jesus, and it felt like we were living Acts 2:46–47:

> And day by day, attending the temple together and breaking bread in their homes, they received their food with glad and generous hearts, praising God and having favor with all the people. And the Lord added to their number day by day those who were being saved. (ESV)

Having established this foundation, we expanded our hospitality as many members of the church opened their homes to sponsor refugees. Our already multiracial church became even more wonderfully diverse. It was messy and sometimes complicated or uncomfortable, but it was very good. Would it have happened without the connections built through hospitality? Probably not.

Getting together at restaurants and coffee shops is great, but something deeper happens when we share our homes. Hospitality doesn't have to be complicated or fancy. Sometimes it's just a cup of coffee and a chance to unwind. My mother taught me this by her example. Now I am thankful to have a home of my own. It's a gift, and God's gifts are meant to be shared, not hoarded. When we open our homes, we are also opening our hearts and allowing people to know us better. They see the pictures on the walls, the books on our shelves, and what our interests are. We share a cup of coffee, or maybe a meal, and we share our lives in the process.

There are times for gourmet cooking and fancy desserts, but a pot of soup and some muffins or bread are easier and can be much more affordable, especially if you're serving a crowd. It's nice to have everything ready when guests arrive, but some of the best times can happen when the company pitches in to finish making the salad or set the table, so I don't worry about having everything perfect. I've also learned that saying yes when someone asks to bring a salad or dessert adds to everyone's pleasure.

So even if all you have to offer is a pot of soup (or a peanut butter and jelly sandwich), invite someone to come home with you today!

MOM'S LENTIL SOUP

This recipe is inspired by my mother's soup but modified to be plant-based (vegan) and gluten free. It is also delicious with barley, or if cooked with chicken stock or with a ham bone for extra flavor.

Serves 6

1 Tbs olive oil
1 med onion, chopped (about 1 cup)
2–4 carrots, chopped (1 cup or more, to taste)
3 or more celery stalks, sliced thinly (include leaves if possible)
1–2 med potatoes, diced (optional)
1–2 cloves garlic, minced

1 cup green or brown lentils or lentil/ barley mix
6 cups water or chicken stock
salt and pepper to taste
1 bay leaf
½ (6 oz) can tomato paste (optional; can also use diced tomatoes or about a cup of leftover spaghetti sauce)

1. In a large pot, add olive oil over medium heat. Add onion, carrots, celery, potatoes (if using), and garlic. Cook for a few minutes, stirring frequently.

2. Add lentils and stir. Immediately add 6 cups water or stock, salt, pepper, and bay leaf.

3. Lower the heat to a gentle simmer and cook for about 1 hour.

4. If desired, add tomato paste or other tomatoes.

5. Taste to see if you need more salt. Add more water if the soup is too thick (note: barley soaks up more liquid than lentils do). This soup can be made a day ahead—in fact, I think it's even better the next day!

The Baking and Breaking of Bread

KAILA YIM

· · · ·

Jesus said to them, "I am the bread of life; whoever comes to me shall not hunger, and whoever believes in me shall never thirst."

John 6:35 ESV

I purchased my home as a twenty-nine-year-old single woman. I knew I would own a home one day, but I never imagined doing it single. Whatever house I ended up purchasing, a consistent desire across the board for me was to have a space that was warm, cozy, inviting, and safe. I wanted to give my house back to the Father and use it for discipleship and fellowship; to invite others in to feel seen, loved, heard, and known. What I ended up creating was a safe haven for others to travel to, to enjoy a home-cooked meal or baked good in, and to point others back to Jesus, the true and only satisfying Bread of Life.

I sometimes felt self-conscious cooking for others, unsure if they would even like what I had prepared. So I started offering guests the banana bread I always had on hand. Let me be clear: I am no baker. This was the first recipe I came across that felt easy, contained minimal and everyday ingredients, and felt healthy. It was also fun, relaxing, and something I could make my own by adding my own touches. Baking it became a weekly rhythm for me.

I was shocked when nearly an entire loaf was devoured in one morning by the women I hosted for Saturday morning Bible study. I knew, then, that this was going to be "my thing."

I desired not only to practically feed the bodies of others but also feed and nourish their souls through Bible study, fellowship, God's Word, and time spent in prayer for one another. What was once a desire to learn how to bake and do it well became a weekly labor of love with the anticipation of the literal breaking of bread with whoever walked through my front door. I spend time baking bread so I can break bread with those who need a listening ear, those who need friendship and a warmed-up slice of banana bread, and those who need nourishment physically and spiritually.

The love I've poured out from both my hands and my heart hasn't just extended to others but also to myself. As I created rhythms for myself, as someone who lived alone and did a lot of the mundane day-to-day alone, baking in the kitchen became something my own heart and soul needed. It was a way for me to watch ingredients come together to make something I enjoyed and usually wanted more than one slice of. And it pointed me to the true Bread of Life, who always satisfies and never leaves me hungry.

· BANANA BREAD ·

Gluten free and dairy free

Yields 1 loaf

3 overripe bananas
2 cups almond flour
2 eggs

½ tsp salt
2 Tbs vanilla extract
1 Tbs baking powder

Optional ingredients

cinnamon (generous amount)
¼ cup agave or honey

chocolate chips (generous amount)

1. Preheat oven to 325°.
2. Peel bananas and mash in a bowl until smooth.
3. Add almond flour, eggs, salt, vanilla, and baking powder.

4. Stir until all ingredients are mixed well and have the smooth consistency of cake batter.

5. Pour into a nonstick bread pan.

6. Bake for 55–60 minutes or until the whole loaf is golden brown on top.

7. Let it cool completely before cutting into or transferring out of loaf pan.

Quiet the Noise

BETHANY LENDERINK

· · · ·

Come to me, all you who are weary and burdened, and I will give you rest.
Matthew 11:28

It was exactly three months after a major surgery to remove a tumor in my brain, and I was learning that the recovery was going to be even harder than the surgery itself. After months of trying to work, take care of my rambunctious one-year-old puppy, and keep my life from falling apart in the midst of constant illness, I had lost what little strength I had left.

I was supposed to lead an adult Bible study class before church on Sunday, and a fellow class leader asked me if I was willing to share some of my testimony.

"You told me earlier you've really seen God in these last few months since your surgery," she said, referencing a conversation we'd had a few weeks prior.

But on that morning, I didn't feel God's presence. I felt anger at what I perceived as his absence. "I'm sorry," I told her. "I don't think my heart is in the right place to talk about God's faithfulness."

She was quiet for a long moment before saying, "Tell me about it."

We talked for a long time. I told her about the different symptoms I was experiencing in my recovery, about my anger that the tumor had taken so much of my life away from me. I told her how exhausted I was of trying to be strong, of pretending to be grateful about the trials I was experiencing. I told her I felt like God was silent at the time I most needed to hear his voice.

I expected her to try to console me, but instead she just asked, "Can I bring you a meal? I'd like to do that, so you have one less thing to worry about." A few days later, she brought a still-warm container of soup to my house, gave me a hug, and said she'd pray for me.

That moment with my friend taught me something vital about ministry: when someone is walking through life's fires, they don't need to hear me, they need to hear God.

Words fail. They do. We say the wrong things, or we offer up empty platitudes, and the words fail. But maybe the old adage that "actions speak louder than words" is truer than we think. When my friend brought me that meal, she didn't just offer me comfort in the midst of one of my darkest moments. She removed one of the obstacles preventing me from feeling God's presence. Instead of worrying about making a meal, I was able to hold a bowl of soup, let its warmth seep into my hands, and find a moment of peace in a season of chaos.

I think of Elijah when he was hiding from Jezebel in the desert. He prayed to God, "I have had enough, LORD. . . . Take my life" (1 Kings 19:4). And as he slept, God sent him an angel, who woke Elijah and said, "Get up and eat," and brought him bread (vv. 5–6). The angel even added, "for the journey is too much for you" (v. 7). God knew Elijah's trials, and he sent someone to relieve the burden. And maybe that's why, in the stressful times of life, we feel compelled to do the same.

Maybe when someone is walking through the valley, our job is not to offer them words but to offer them our actions. Maybe our job is to relieve them of what burdens we can, to quiet the noise so they can listen to the Father. Maybe our job is not to tell them how to leave the valley or to tell them that we see them but to walk alongside them until God leads them out.

Maybe our job is to provide a meal in the hope it will bring a moment of peace.

The Comfort Food That Seasoned a Forever Friendship

JENNI ELWOOD

. . . .

For God is working in you, giving you the desire and the power to do what pleases him.
Philippians 2:13 NLT

I think our daughters love each other. Can we have a playdate?"

As the birthday party waned, a kind lady spoke these words to me as she waddled over, looking ready to give birth any minute.

I'd watched my three-year-old daughter pair off with a little girl I didn't recognize after entering the packed party room at a pizza place earlier that afternoon. As the event wrapped up, I sought out the other girl's mom so I could ask her the same thing—but she beat me to it.

"Once that baby arrives, I'll bring your family a meal," I replied. After chatting for a few minutes, we pried our daughters apart, exchanged phone numbers, and awaited the new baby's grand entrance.

After their family was settled back at home after an uncomplicated birth, I pondered which comfort food to assemble in the kitchen. I landed on a combination of a rich tomato base, an array of south-of-the-border spices, and a diversity of textures. So I made a big pot of savory chili to nourish her family for days.

We all appreciate good hospitality, don't we? More than once I've delivered store-bought food to friends in the midst of a struggle, and it's appreciated.

But crafting delicious food uniquely blesses others. Sometimes it's necessary to set aside hectic schedules and construct a hearty meal from scratch.

And this was one of those times.

Instead of grabbing frozen lasagna from a cardboard box, I sifted through my recipes until I came across the perfect one. My sister-in-law had treated our family to bowls of chili a while back that blew our minds, and thankfully I spied the photocopy from her tucked into one of my vintage recipe boxes.

When we consider the root of hospitality, we could go shallow and consider ourselves the ones doing it all. It's tempting to think we behave in a way that pleases God by chance. But if we go deeper and examine Scripture to discover where our motives come from, our key verse from Philippians illuminates a few things.

In the first part of the verse, we see God working. In the original Greek, this kind of "work" is not mundane but implies a miraculous context. At times, we struggle to find God moving in the midst of everyday tasks like feeding our families. But sacred moments motivated by God's work come through us from the kindness of our compassionate God. This isn't accomplished on our own but through his desire and power.

In the latter half of the verse, when the work God accomplishes in us takes hold, we are given "the desire and the power to do what pleases him." The word translated "pleases" also means "good purpose," "kind-intentioned," and "filled with delight." God's good purpose roots out attributes such as self-centeredness that might prevent us from serving others well.

His kind delight worked through us brings a deeper meaning to the "comfort" in comfort food.

I love that it pleases him to nourish new mamas and their young families with a delicious bowl of chili. When my daughter and I knocked on the door for our playdate, with piping hot soup sending forth the aroma of rosemary and cumin, we entered a sweet house full of love and friendship that continues to bless us to this day.

Friends, let's live surrendered to the call of serving others well. You never know when living out God's good purpose will bring the gift of deep relationship that lasts into eternity. We can trust God will help us live fully engaged with intention, bringing comfort to others.

SAVORY COMFORT CHILI TO SHARE WITH FRIENDS

Serves 18

3 lbs ground beef
3 med onions, chopped
10 celery stalks, chopped
2 (28 oz) cans diced tomatoes, undrained
4 (16 oz) cans mixed beans, drained and rinsed
1 (32 oz) box tomato soup (any variety you desire)

3 cups beef stock
3 Tbs chili powder
1 heaping Tbs kosher salt
2 heaping Tbs minced garlic
1 (6 oz) can tomato paste
1 Tbs pepper
1 Tbs each cumin, thyme, oregano, and rosemary
½ tsp cayenne pepper

1. In a large soup pot, cook beef, onions, and celery over medium heat until meat is fully cooked. Drain any excess liquid.

2. Add all remaining ingredients to the pot and mix together on high heat until it begins to boil, stirring occasionally. Once bubbling, taste to make sure the flavor is to your liking and adjust spices as necessary.

3. Turn down to low and simmer for 1 hour.

Serve with a dollop of sour cream, a sprinkle of cheddar, and a loaf of French bread or corn chips as an accompaniment.

Inviting Others
to the Table

NAOMI ZYLSTRA

. . . .

When God's people are in need, be ready to help them. Always be eager to practice hospitality.

Romans 12:13 NLT

My husband's favorite food is pizza. He doesn't discriminate between humble frozen pizza or gourmet brick oven pizza. When we got married, his favorite item on our registry was a pizza oven that we now keep on our deck. Making pizzas for family and friends quickly became our go-to form of hospitality, whether we're having a few friends over or feeding my parents after they help us remove wallpaper.

The thing I love about pizza is that it can appeal to almost everyone's preferences. It's difficult to find someone who doesn't like any pizza. And pizza is shareable. It's even served in slices, ready to be dished out.

When it comes to having people over, hospitality and food are deeply connected. I recently had family over, and my sister scolded me for checking in with everyone too much. I know how uncomfortable it can be to ask a busy host for a glass of water, or to crack a window, so I want to anticipate my guests' needs. And I know that each guest has different tastes and preferences.

Sharing food as hospitality is certainly not a new concept. When Jesus knew that he had only a short while left to live, he chose to eat a meal with his friends. He emphasized the importance of his renewed covenant with the disciples through food and drink. This also gave his friends a chance to talk together one more time before Jesus went to Calvary.

Seeing Jesus taking time to eat with his closest friends shows how important food can be when it comes to practicing Christian community. When Christians eat together, it is a reminder that we all share the same set of basic needs like food, clothes, and shelter. It's also a reminder that our community can help provide for those needs. Within sharing a meal is the statement of understanding and providing a person's daily need for food.

For Christians, eating in a community setting and sharing a meal such as pizza can seem so innocuous, but the act can actually have a deep spiritual meaning. Having pizza together tells another person that you know and understand their need for food, and you want to show love to them by meeting that hunger at its most basic level. People "hunger" for all sorts of things, but only when our basic needs are met can we go on to pursue higher callings.

Jesus demonstrated this concept of meeting a person's basic needs and therefore allowing them to grow. When Jesus found himself in a crowd after a long sermon, he didn't send the people away. He knew what it meant to be hungry. And he knew that a hungry stomach could negate any retention of the sermon he'd just preached. Jesus understood the human reality of needing dinner and used this need for food to bless the people rather than pushing through the hunger to try to teach them more. When Jesus fed the five thousand, he gave us a glimpse of the hospitality and abundance we will get to experience in the new creation.

So even though sharing food within a community sounds simple and casual, it's really building deeper connections between the people sharing it. Hospitality through food is a way of showing that a person's basic needs are cared for. It also allows for growth when a person's sole focus isn't on their next meal. I know from personal experience that when I know dinner is taken care of already, I can shift my mind to focus on personal growth or even how I can better serve the people around me.

PIZZA FOR A CROWD

Yields 6 pizzas

For the crust

pizza dough for 6 (14-inch) pizzas,
  homemade or purchased

For the sauce

1 (28 oz) can San Marzano tomatoes
4 lg cloves garlic
½ tsp salt
¼ tsp pepper
2 Tbs olive oil

1 Tbs honey
1½ Tbs shredded Parmesan cheese
1 tsp dried parsley
1 tsp dried oregano

For topping

24 oz each mozzarella, provolone,
  and Monterey Jack cheese (or your
  preferred blend), shredded

suggested toppings: pepperoni, sausage,
  ham, prosciutto, onions, mushrooms,
  peppers, olives, roasted garlic

1. Preheat oven to 425° or according to dough instructions.

2. Blend all sauce ingredients in food processor or blender in 30-second increments until combined, around 1 minute total.

3. Using your hands or a rolling pin, roll out dough for each pizza crust to approximately 12–14 inches in diameter, or desired thinness.

4. Ladle sauce onto dough in a thin, even layer, leaving an inch around the edge.

5. Evenly sprinkle on cheese until sauce is no longer visible.

6. Top pizzas with your choice of toppings.

7. Bake pizzas in oven according to dough instructions, or until cheese is melted and bubbly and crust has a golden bottom, about 12–18 minutes.

8. Slice each pizza into eight pieces and enjoy!

Just Enough for Noah

DONNA PRYOR

· · · ·

Do not forget to show hospitality to strangers, for by so doing some people have shown hospitality to angels without knowing it.

Hebrews 13:2

While we were growing up, my father often told us stories of his childhood. He was raised in rural Mississippi in the 1940s. His family was poor. His father was a sharecropper, and my father spent most of his childhood picking cotton. As I reflect on my father's stories in my old age, his stories help me to understand who he was and why he did the things he did.

One of the stories my father told most often was about his visit to Ms. Ann's house. As he told it, he and his mother had walked to town, and on the way back home they stopped at Ms. Ann's house. I never figured out if Ms. Ann was a relative or just a family friend. He also never said why they stopped. When they got there, Ms. Ann was frying fish. My father and grandmother had been out all day and had walked far. My father was hungry. The look on his face when he described how good that fish smelled frying up in that cast-iron skillet let you know he remembered it as if it were yesterday. I'm sure that, as a young boy, he didn't know how to hide the anticipation on his face as he awaited the taste of fish, hot out of the grease, in his mouth. Ms. Ann must have sensed his desire and declared, as she took the fish out of the skillet, "It's just enough for Noah."

Noah was Ms. Ann's husband. With that one sentence, Ms. Ann let my father and grandmother know that she had nothing to offer them to eat. They would have to find relief from their long journey elsewhere. All she had was designated for her husband, and she had nothing to spare.

This experience had a profound effect on my father. When he grew up and secured his own home, he made sure there was always enough food in the house for us and anyone else who happened to show up. There was always something to offer. Whether he knew you had a need, or he was just being neighborly, no one ever left our house hungry. I can only imagine the heartbreak he felt as he walked home, stomach growling, the smell of fried fish still lingering in his nostrils.

That was rural Mississippi in the 1940s. I can sympathize with Ms. Ann a bit. I'm sure their financial situation was not much better than my grandparents'. Fast-forward to the present day. Many of us live in homes with rooms that go unused and live next to neighbors we do not know. An unexpected guest can easily be ignored, thanks to our video doorbell systems. It is hard for many of us to live out the spirit of Hebrews 13:2 because we live life in silos, only interacting with a select group of people we know and understand and who know and understand us.

Let us move into a new season of welcoming guests to our tables. Tables that are not just full of food but of laughter and love. Tables where memories are created and treasured for a lifetime. Tables where souls are nourished just as much as stomachs. Cheerfully share your home with those who need a meal or a place to stay today.

Friends of the Soul

SHELLY SULFRIDGE

. . . .

God is not unjust; he will not forget your work and the love you have shown him as you have helped his people and continue to help them.

Hebrews 6:10

Transplants to Alaska don't always stay long. In a place where the temperature drops to sixty below, we've grown used to that. However, some moves hurt more than others. When one of my close friends recently left, I grieved. This was a friend I could depend on. She delivered soup to my door when I was sick and was someone I could count on for prayer.

As the time drew closer for her to leave, we said our goodbyes. At first, I wasn't too sad because she promised to spend time here every summer. But as I watched her make her way down the road, it hit me. I cried hard. I asked my husband, "Who will bring me soup when I'm sick?"

Every time one of us was sick, we brought soup to the other. Who would take her soup now? I texted her and told her I would pray that God would send someone to bring her soup when she was sick.

As a missionary who ministers to the native people in the surrounding villages, when someone is in their last days or passes away, I have been taught by the native people to show up at their homes and cook with the family, share stories, and visit. Time is so much more important to them than dropping off soup and leaving. But I grew up in the South, where taking soup is a custom, and I miss that too.

Jesus often uses meals to engage with people. We can learn so much by reading about his encounters with others around the table. He uses this time to counsel and fellowship with them.

In my new culture, it's not about the food served or how many courses; it's about fellowship. Food can bring us together no matter our culture.

In the Sermon on the Mount, Jesus says, "Give, and it will be given to you. A good measure, pressed down, shaken together and running over, will be poured into your lap. For with the measure you use, it will be measured to you" (Luke 6:38).

Dropping off soup to someone who doesn't feel like visiting or spending time with someone who just needs company on their worst day will not only bring them joy but also bring us fulfillment and comfort. If we follow Jesus's example, we will be a step ahead.

A few days after my friend left, I got sick. Imagine my joy, tears, and surprise when another friend dropped off a pot of soup at my door. I had a feeling my soup friend had prayed the same prayer for me that I had prayed for her—that someone new would bring the soup.

God sends us what we need right when we need it. Not that my body needed soup that day; after all, we had leftover stew my husband had made the day before. My soul needed the thought that someone cared. And I felt like God was saying, *You're never alone. Even when your friend moves away, she's still your friend, and you have other friends. But most of all, you have me: your forever friend and provider.*

Sometimes the situation requires us to stay and minister. Sometimes it's better to drop off food and leave the person to rest, but whatever your culture of reaching out may have taught you, you will be a blessing to someone.

COUNTRY VEGETABLE SOUP

Serves 6–8

1 lb ground beef
2 (14.5 oz) cans diced tomatoes
1 (15 oz) can tomato sauce
2 (15 oz) cans whole kernel corn,
 drained
1 (14.5 oz) can green beans, drained

2 (15 oz) cans diced potatoes, drained
1 sm onion, chopped
2 celery stalks, chopped
1½ tsp salt
1 tsp pepper

1. In a large pot, brown ground beef until cooked through and then drain.

2. Add all remaining ingredients to the pot. Bring to a boil, then simmer for thirty minutes.

The Grand Illusion

RHONDA STOPPE

· · · ·

And my God will meet all your needs according to the riches of his glory in Christ Jesus.

Philippians 4:19

S ure, I'd love to have you drop by for dessert," I said while looking at our chaotic mess.

I wanted our home to be a place where people felt welcome, but in reality, whenever we invited someone over, a sense of panic arose from the depth of my soul. It's not that I didn't like having people over. I loved it. But what I didn't like was how I felt pressed to turn my lived-in home into an HGTV display of loveliness.

On this particular day, I frantically did a clean sweep. I threw toys into baskets, stuffed blankets into closets, and used the kitchen towel to wipe down the counter and dust the coffee table.

With this scramble came no time to bake a dessert. Maybe you've been there. You know, when you have only enough time to bake or clean—but not both. Since I didn't want to do the walk of shame while escorting our guests through a messy house, I opted to clean.

Then, in the few moments I had left, I scanned the cupboards to discover what I could use to create a dessert. And there it was. In all its glory. A store-bought angel food cake. You know, that small circle that gets kind of rubbery if not eaten right away. And is only enjoyable if it is smothered in strawberries and whipped cream. Alas, I had no fruit or cream. But I did have some of the kids' prepackaged chocolate pudding cups.

I thought to myself, *Hmmm . . . what can I do with these?*

I quickly grabbed the dental floss. Yes, that's what I said, *dental floss.* I used a strand of floss to cut horizontally across the middle of the cake. Once it was in two pieces, I spread a container of pudding onto the bottom half of the cake. Then I replaced the top.

So far, so good.

But the cake was still lacking; the top layer was sort of slipping off the layer of pudding. Then I remembered my mother-in-law's amazing chocolate frosting recipe. *Do I have cocoa powder? And powdered sugar? Please tell me I have some powdered sugar stashed somewhere.*

"Yes! There it is," I said out loud in victory.

Quickly I melted some butter in a microwave safe bowl and added the cocoa powder and powdered sugar. With a hand mixer, I began to combine the ingredients, adding tiny splashes of milk until it began to take on the consistency of frosting.

Once I spread the frosting on the cake, I was inspired to stretch my creativity a bit further. I found a chocolate bar in my secret stash of "Mom's goody drawer." Just as our guests arrived, I pulled out the cheese grater and shredded chocolate over the top of the freshly spread frosting. It was glorious. So pretty. And finished just in the nick of time!

When the coffee was brewed, we gathered in the kitchen to enjoy the most amazing fellowship. Oh, how I almost missed out on this time of community because I was afraid my hospitality wasn't on par. I was worried about food and drink when I should have been concerned with the people God was allowing us to serve.

The cake was delicious—although I did have to steady it and use a very sharp serrated knife to cut it into slices. And when our guests asked for the recipe for the yummy dessert, we all had a good laugh when I came clean with the frantic way I'd assembled it.

God calls us to use our homes to entertain strangers. He wants you and me to humbly share what he's blessed us with to encourage community. How easily we go astray when our fear over not measuring up to others' expectations keeps us from opening our homes! I pray that this story will inspire you to not be anxious about what you will eat but rather be ready whenever God gives you an opportunity to share his hospitality with others.

CHOCOLATE FROSTING

¼ cup butter (½ stick)
2 Tbs cocoa powder

1 cup powdered sugar
¼ cup milk

1. In a microwave safe bowl, melt the butter.

2. Stir cocoa powder into the melted butter. Add ¼ cup of powdered sugar. Mix together with hand mixer on low until smooth.

3. Add about 1 Tbs milk and continue mixing. Continue adding powdered sugar ¼ cup at a time, alternating with milk, until it is your desired consistency. Don't make the frosting too wet, or it won't stick to the sides of the cake. If you do add too much milk, you can always add more powdered sugar to thicken.

The Sweetest Gift

JESSICA MATHISEN

· · · ·

For the bread of God is he who comes down from heaven and gives life to the world.
John 6:33 ESV

The year my third child came into the world, everything around me seemed to be caving in as loss after loss piled up and threatened to steal my joy. It was the hardest year yet of my adult life. Job loss, foster parenting, secondary trauma, strained relationships, and financial uncertainty took their toll. How would I be able to bring another child into a life that felt full of sorrow?

During that season of unrelenting grief, the body of Christ was the hands and feet of Jesus as they held us up. One day, a friend reached out to me to ask if she could bring us dinner. When I told her we had meals covered for the week, she texted back, "How about fresh eggs and a loaf of homemade bread on Wednesday morning?" I quickly replied, "That sounds amazing! Thank you!"

As promised, two days later there was a loaf of bread on my front porch and a bag of fresh eggs from her chicken coop. Tears welled up in my eyes as I opened the bag and saw that she had packaged the loaf with twine, complete with a tiny spool of golden thread and a note that read, "May you see the goodness of God in the golden threads of your story." The intentionality and kindness of this friend overwhelmed me.

And the crazy part was, this was a friend I had met maybe twice. But the love of Christ compelled her to reach out and to share what she had—a loaf of bread and some farm fresh eggs. It was a gesture of kindness I will never forget.

In Acts 2, we read about the New Testament church and their means of providing for one another through acts of generosity and kindness. Scripture

227

tells us of the beautiful fellowship they enjoyed with one another: "And day by day, attending the temple together and breaking bread in their homes, they received their food with glad and generous hearts, praising God and having favor with all the people" (Acts 2:46–47 ESV).

After an incredibly traumatic season filled with many losses and transitions, I made it my goal to learn to bake my own homemade sourdough. I wanted to be able to bless others in the way my friend had blessed me. The joy of making sourdough has been a blessing not only to my family, who enjoy a fresh loaf (or two!) every week, but also to numerous friends and family members.

Sourdough has proven to be the sweetest gift to give in nearly any situation:

welcoming a new baby
celebrating a birthday
offering congratulations for a new job
grieving a loss
just because

Isn't this the life we long for—to be cared for by others and know that God is caring for us through the kindness of others? God created us with a need for others. We were not made to do life alone. Within our hearts is the desire to be seen and understood by people who will carry us when we cannot bring ourselves to the Father. People who will pray for us when we have run out of prayers to pray.

This desire to be seen and understood by others points to our heart's deepest desire—to be known and loved by God himself. The beautiful thing is that God has made himself available to us as the Bread of Life. While sourdough bread is arguably one of the best comfort foods, we can rest assured in knowing that God is the God of all comfort. He is our refuge and will satisfy and sustain us. He is the Bread of Life, broken for us so that we would be able to know his peace, no matter what brokenness we face.

He knows when you are weary, tired, broken, and confused. He sees each tear you cry. And he knows which prayers you have given up on praying. But he is there, ready to satisfy your every hunger and thirst with himself.

The Recipe for Soul Care

Unexpected Provision

BRIANNA DEWITT

. . . .

When the dew was gone, thin flakes like frost on the ground appeared on the desert floor. When the Israelites saw it, they said to each other, "What is it?" For they did not know what it was. Moses said to them, "It is the bread the LORD has given you to eat."

Exodus 16:14–15

As a bearer of a large sweet tooth, I've enjoyed baking for as long as I can remember—partly for the process but also very much for the results. When I baked as a kid with my grandma or tried things at home, I had family members around to enjoy the end result, or maybe I'd bring the cookies or muffins to school with me.

As my life circumstances changed, though, it became tricky that most dessert recipes make an awful lot. From a three-layer cake to four dozen cookies, the scale of most recipes was simply much larger than I actually needed. I'd find myself wanting to make something, but if I didn't have a place to bring a large quantity of dessert, I'd end up simply not baking at all. I didn't want any of it to go to waste if I kept it at home and tried to work through it by myself or with the occasional friend stopping by.

I don't remember what helped me find it (though if I had to guess, I'd say Pinterest was likely involved), but one day I came across a website that seemed to understand my dilemma. It was filled with recipes for six cookies, or four muffins, or cheesecakes made in six-inch pans. I had found a way to fulfill my enjoyment of making desserts without making way more than I needed. There were times when a recipe sounded good but wasn't feasible because I didn't have the correct (small) size pan or container, but over several years I've built up a collection of small pans, pie plates, and more. Now, when a friend is coming over and we want just a little bit of dessert, or I simply feel like baking, I'm able to do so at a level that's fitting and not wasteful.

Scaling a recipe down or up to feed a different size crowd may not be a hugely novel concept, but the discovery that other people had successfully created smaller-sized recipes started to give me the courage to begin playing with recipes too.

For a long time, I took these small recipes for granted, but the more I've thought about it, the more I've come to see it as a bit of manna that God has given me. When the Israelites started to complain about not having enough to eat in the desert after leaving Egypt, God graced them with an answer—manna. Yet the first time they saw "thin flakes like frost" covering the ground, they didn't understand what it was. As Moses explained, it was food for them, but it was only good for that day. God's provision was just what they needed it to be.

The ability to make small batches of dessert is not nearly as important as the kind of sustenance the Israelites received, but the underlying idea is the same: God is a provider. For the Israelites, they needed him to provide their very literally daily bread—they wouldn't have survived in the desert without it. Small-sized desserts are by no means critical to life (though they sure are tasty!), yet they allow me to experience the enjoyment of baking in a way that's better suited to how my life looks.

If we overlook these small graces, we run the risk of starting to overlook the big ones too. The more I look for them, the more I begin to see God's small ways of providing for me all around. It might be in the shape of a well-timed text from a friend, a Sunday sermon that seems specifically tailored to my current circumstances—or even a recipe for a small dessert.

SMALL BATCH CHOCOLATE PEANUT BUTTER OATMEAL BARS

*If you don't have a square container close to the right size,
a similar sized bowl works great too.*

Yields 4 bars

1½ Tbs butter
1½ heaping Tbs peanut butter
1 heaping Tbs brown sugar
¼ tsp vanilla

⅛ tsp salt
½ cup rolled oats (quick cooking oats
 will not create the optimal texture)
¼ cup chocolate chips

1. Mix butter, peanut butter, brown sugar, vanilla, and salt in a small saucepan over low heat until butter is melted and everything is incorporated.

2. Add oats to the pan and continue to cook for approximately 2 minutes. Remove from heat.

3. Pour mixture into a square container about 5×5 and flatten.

4. In a small bowl, melt chocolate chips in the microwave and spread over the oatmeal mixture.

5. Refrigerate until set, then cut into 4 pieces.

Jam Church

LINDSEY SPOOLSTRA

. . . .

Whoever sows to please their flesh, from the flesh will reap destruction; whoever sows to please the Spirit, from the Spirit will reap eternal life. Let us not become weary in doing good, for at the proper time we will reap a harvest if we do not give up.

Galatians 6:8–9

Don't worry, this devotion isn't really about the pandemic. It just begins there.

Flash back with me to spring 2020—my office is closed, my church is closed, and stay-at-home orders are in place. I live alone, and 97 percent of my human interaction is gone. It's a time of uncertainty and of active resistance against anxiety and fearmongering and loneliness and the desire to overbuy toilet paper. I'm eager to find ways to stay positive and *do something*, not just wring my hands and watch people lose their minds and their jobs. So my watchword for the year becomes *patience*, and I go so far as to paint a big sign to that effect for my front porch. With flowers on it.

I don't have to tell you how weird things got in 2020. You know.

By summertime, things had stabilized a bit, though church and work remained virtual. I'd created some new habits and worked on being both patient and flexible. I was struggling with "attending church" via YouTube, though. Okay, I'll be honest: I wasn't watching. I felt guilty, but staring at a little screen was not doing a thing for me.

I needed to find a better way. Enter Jam Church.

Here in West Michigan, summertime is *all the fruit* time, and I'm always eager to celebrate it. And pick it. And eat it. And make jams and chutneys and sauces and salsas with it. From May (rhubarb) to October (wild grapes), my kitchen is reliably in some stage of home preserving. (And don't even get me started on tomatoes.)

I could not sit and watch church. But I could stand at my stove over my jam pot and watch fruit turn into a gloriously jewel-toned spread with a worship song on my lips and a sermon in my earbuds and my hands busily practicing a skill they knew so well. Active. Energizing. Soothing. Productive. Simple.

Was I "failing" to worship the Lord?

I admit my focus was not 100 percent. (But let's be honest—that is not a symptom only of virtual church.) However, I showed up. I tuned in. My Sunday morning church space, snatched away by my own distraction by the weird world, came back. Glory, hallelujah, and pectin.

There's a beautiful rhythm in the growing season. It is generally predictable —rhubarb before strawberries before cherries before peaches—but not rigid. No two years are identical. No two crops are the same. No two batches of jam are identical.

And that is well.

How can we celebrate abundance without times of scarcity? How can we appreciate the rhythms of daily life without their disruption? How can we realize what really matters without space—voluntarily sought or otherwise—to step free of the clutter?

How can we celebrate our God-given ability to flex and adapt without having to do so? We are creative. We are unique. We are *not* in control. We are workers in the harvest, plucking the fruit of seed others planted and God caused to grow.

> On each side of the river stood the tree of life, bearing twelve crops of fruit, yielding its fruit every month. And the leaves of the tree are for the healing of the nations. (Rev. 22:2)

JAMMY GRANOLA BARS

This recipe is highly flexible, is easy to double, and can accommodate all sorts of dietary modifications. Adapted from Fresh Off The Grid.

Yields 6 bars

1½ cups rolled oats
½ cup jam of choice
¼ cup nut butter of choice

1 Tbs coconut oil
¼ tsp salt (optional)
¼ cup chopped nuts (optional)

1. Preheat oven to 350°. Oil a 9×5 loaf pan or line with parchment paper or foil, leaving overhang on the long sides.

2. Optional step: toast the oats on a rimmed baking sheet for about 10 minutes, stirring halfway through, until fragrant and beginning to color. Remove from the oven and set aside.

3. In a small saucepan over medium heat, combine jam, nut butter, coconut oil, and salt, if using, and simmer for about 3 minutes or until slightly thickened, stirring constantly.

4. Remove pan from heat and add oats. Stir to thoroughly combine.

5. Spread mixture into prepared loaf pan. Sprinkle chopped nuts on the top, if using, and press down lightly.

6. Bake for 15 minutes, until golden brown. Allow to cool completely before cutting into bars either in the pan or, using the overhanging foil or parchment, after lifting the bars from the pan.

* Fresh Off The Grid, "Peanut Butter & Jelly Granola Bars," Fresh Off The Grid, accessed November 27, 2023, https://www.freshoffthegrid.com/peanut-butter-jelly-granola-bars/#recipe.

Life's Essentials

ESSIE FAYE TAYLOR

. . . .

Therefore I tell you, do not worry about your life, what you will eat or drink; or about your body, what you will wear. Is not life more than food, and the body more than clothes?

Matthew 6:25

As I reminisce about good times in my past, a few things are staples: noise, love, faith, laughter, and food. And not entirely in that order. In my mind's eye, I envision how these elements created a warm and welcoming space that I called home. I'm one of fifteen siblings reared in the South Side neighborhood of Inglewood in Chicago, Illinois. We were fortunate to receive love, faith, and provision in a warm and welcoming home environment. At nearly every significant occasion that I remember, these elements were present, and I was "home."

Regardless of whether I attended a joyous occasion like a wedding or a heartbreaking loss and simultaneous celebration, like a homegoing, I was "home" because of the presence of these staples. They have a calming energy and transformative power. Each element is steeped in the cultural tradition into which I was born. This experience is a part of me, and I carry it wherever I find myself.

As believers, faith is an essential element of our daily walk. Worry is something we are to cast aside—as a matter of fact, we are to cast our worries (our cares) on the Lord, because he cares for us (1 Pet. 5:7). He exchanges our worries for faith and confidence that he will provide for our needs and take care of our concerns. In today's text, the Lord Jesus Christ assures his listeners of life's essentials. This includes food for the body and the soul. Jesus admonishes believers not to worry because God provides for the sparrow, which gives no thought to its needs. Of course he will provide for humanity, his masterpiece.

Jesus's discourse includes food as an essential element of life, and he underscores the importance of nourishing our bodies with proper nutrition and care. Though he does not discount the importance of food, Jesus also declares that life's essentials exceed what we see in this physical world: our physical bodies and clothes. The spiritual realm, including feeding our souls, is essential. Soul care is of eternal importance.

Feeding the soul consists of both independent and communal disciplines. Independent disciplines include personal devotion, fasting, meditation upon God's Word, and application of biblical principles within daily living. Communal disciplines include attending corporate worship and community prayer and Bible study groups. We learn and grow in our faith communities. We build partnerships and exchange ideas as we grow together and serve God and others side by side. Both types of spiritual disciplines create a sense of "home": safety and strength.

Jesus is the perfect instructor of this lesson. He is the perfect contradiction: God in human flesh. He is sinless yet wrapped in sinful humanity. He is fully God and fully man. As a result, he is our High Priest who understands the human experience. He has walked in our shoes yet brings salvation to humankind through his incredible sacrifice.

Essential to life are physical nourishment and nourishment of the soul. Holiness includes maintaining the delicate balance of both as we walk with God in this present world; Jesus is our perfect example.

Call to action:

1. Acknowledge that nourishing the body with food, self-care, and healthy relationships is essential to life.
2. Prioritize feeding your soul with daily spiritual disciplines and living out your faith through biblical principles.

3. Live a holy life; don't be "so heavenly minded that you're of no earthly good," as the saying goes. But also, don't be so mindful of life on earth that you neglect the reality of eternity.
4. Create "home" in every space in which you find yourself. Make room for love, safety, and peace—the transformative power of God—in the simple day-to-day events.
5. Remember, we are the light of the world. It is our responsibility to bring hope to a dying world.

Girl Dinner

HELEN ARNOLD

· · · ·

For he satisfies the thirsty and fills the hungry with good things.
Psalm 107:9

There is no food that quite satisfies my soul like a girl dinner. *Girl dinner* is a friendly term for a meal that basically consists of snacks, appetizers, and small portions of your favorite random foods . . . all on one plate.

Personally, my girl dinner includes chips layered with chunky and creamy guacamole. And I'm rather partial to a mini cheese board: thick and runny Brie drizzled with honey on crackers and a slab of cheddar with chutney on fresh, crunchy bread. Add a handful of roasted pistachios and cut-up watermelon to put a bit of color on my plate and—poof!—my willpower disappears as I focus on the goodness in front of me.

My husband is rather partial to girl dinners too. However, he leaves out the fruit and adds a selection of his favorite cured meats. When the weather is nice, we take our plates and sit on comfy chairs in the yard overlooking the lavender and rose bushes. Together, we enjoy the feast in front of us. For a while, there's silence as we dig into our meal. Then, in between bites, we share our days: th Sometimes it's the companion as well as the meal that fills up our souls. things that went well . . . and didn't go so well. We talk about our kids, each other, work, church, and what's happening in the world.

In Song of Songs, the allegory tells us a story of Jesus's relationship with us. It says:

> I have come into my garden, my sister, my bride;
> I have gathered my myrrh with my spice.

I have eaten my honeycomb and my honey;
   I have drunk my wine and my milk.
Eat, friends, and drink;
   drink your fill of love. (Song 5:1)

Sitting with Jesus in his garden—whether that be our comfy chair, stretched out on the sofa, or at the kitchen table with a cup of tea in hand—we are invited to eat and drink until we are full. He doesn't say "come and eat the foods you don't like" or "limit yourself to what you need." Jesus invites us to eat our favorite dinner with him.

It would be easy to focus on just the delicious meal in this passage. Yet, he also says, "I have gathered my myrrh with my spice." Traditionally, myrrh is used in the treatment of wounds and to reduce aches, inflammation, obesity, and gastrointestinal pain. It takes time in the garden to harvest myrrh. Cuts are made into its gnarly bark, and a translucent resin slowly seeps out, just like the nails that were hammered into Jesus's hands and feet released a flow of crimson blood.

After the cuts have been scored onto the myrrh's bark, the gardener must wait two to three weeks for the resin to harden before it can be scraped off to use to treat the wounds of people. But once harvested, the wound on the tree reopens and more goodness flows out. This process happens repeatedly, thus providing a continual supply. Likewise, when Jesus shed his blood for us, it tended our wounds as his children. And his healing never runs out. There's enough for all who need it, and he provides it at his dinner table.

When Jesus invites you to eat and drink, all you must decide is, Will you enter his garden? If so, he promises you your favorite foods and time with the One who knows and loves you more than anyone else in this world. And as you sit, Jesus refreshes your soul, tends your wounds, and quenches your thirst with his love.

Have you joined him for dinner in the garden recently? How was your soul refreshed?

Do you have any wounds that need tending?

Sweet Retreat

AMY NEMECEK

· · · · ·

There remains, then, a Sabbath-rest for the people of God; for anyone who enters God's rest also rests from their works, just as God did from his. Let us, therefore, make every effort to enter that rest.

Hebrews 4:9–11

I've waited a whole long Sunday afternoon for this. I'm standing on a kitchen chair beside my dad. He's at the stove, stirring sugar and milk and peanut butter in a saucepan. My eyes are almost level with his sandpaper chin. His schoolboy cowlick, which had been neatly slicked in place for church this morning, gave up trying to behave since Dad's afternoon nap.

This is the only time I remember seeing my dad work in the kitchen. But what he's doing is magic—taking simple ingredients and turning them into a playful treat. This is our family's Sabbath day, when we take a break from our ordinary everyday activities. And Dad's Sunday afternoon peanut butter fudge is all part of the fun.

My sister butters a pie plate. Dad keeps the wooden spoon moving in a figure eight. I watch the red line on the candy thermometer clipped to the lip of the pan. It's my job to tell Dad when it reaches the exact mark he pointed to. The red goes up . . . up . . . up, and if I blink, we might overshoot the mark. The closer that line gets, the more impatient I become. To a five-year-old, those last few degrees take forever, but finally—time!

Dad slides the pan off the burner and begins beating the fudge with Mom's eggbeater. The kind with a hand crank that turns the gear that makes the twin beaters spin. So very steampunk. Dad turns that crank until the fudge becomes creamy, and then he pours it into the pie plate.

I scrape out the pan and lick the spoon, burning my tongue to get an early taste because I know Dad will wait to cut the fudge until it's almost cool. My siblings and I line up at the counter as Dad pries squares of delicious sweetness from the pan and hands them to us. Such a simple, playful treat that makes our Sabbath sweet.

My parents followed the letter of the law by keeping the Sabbath holy. But they also followed the spirit of the law by keeping it playful. I wish I could say I've consistently carried that practice through to adulthood since the sugar highs of Dad's fudge. It hasn't always been easy, though.

During the years my husband worked in full-time pastoral ministry, the Sabbath was often anything but sweet. Or playful. When we finally got to go home after a busy day at church, we didn't feel at all refreshed and wanted nothing more than a nap. And then we figured out that Sabbath doesn't have to equal Sunday. The word itself simply means "to rest." In the opening chapter of Genesis, God creates the world in six days, and on the seventh day he "sabbaths." He enjoys the sweet pleasure of all he has made, and he invites us to join him in that generous act of rest and play and delight.

Sounds pretty good, right? Or maybe you're thinking it sounds impossible. I get it.

My husband and I began to intentionally set aside Fridays as a day dedicated to delight. Usually that meant we stayed home and relaxed. I would take a long walk on our country road. We might take our son out for pizza or barbecue or ice cream. Maybe watch a baseball game or go see a movie. It didn't have to be anything spectacular or costly. We were together, and the gift of being present to one another was a sweet treat.

This week, try setting apart a day to rest from your everyday responsibilities and delight in God's good gifts. It may be hard at first, but by incorporating this rhythm into your week, you'll soon look forward to a whole day to "taste and see that the LORD is good" (Ps. 34:8).

SUNDAY AFTERNOON PEANUT BUTTER FUDGE

Yields 64 1-inch squares (1 serving equals 2 squares)

2 cups sugar
2 Tbs creamy peanut butter
½ cup milk

½ tsp vanilla extract
butter for pan

1. In a 1-quart saucepan, combine sugar, peanut butter, and milk. Cook over medium heat, stirring constantly, until the mixture reaches 240° on a candy thermometer (soft ball stage).

2. Remove pan from heat and add vanilla. Using a hand mixer, beat the fudge on medium-low until creamy, about 2 minutes.

3. Pour into a buttered 8×8 pan and allow to cool. When almost cool (but still a little warm), cut into 1-inch squares. Enjoy!

A Meal of Forgiveness

ANDREA DOERING

. . . .

Better a dry crust eaten in peace than a house filled with feasting —and conflict.
Proverbs 17:1 NLT

Proverbs 17:1 was, unfortunately, a verse that described my feelings about meals with my mother-in-law for much of our relationship. Conflict and strife never seemed too far from the surface, and if we got through a family meal unscathed, it felt like a miracle. It was certainly an answer to prayer. Still, it always felt like a close-run thing.

She liked to host family meals, which put her in control. For the same reason, I liked to host. This relationship didn't bring out the best in me. I had grown up in a family of peaceful meals, and I bitterly resented what was acceptable and conveyed to our children through these contentious family meals. We might have continued on this way for decades, if God hadn't used a meal shared at neither home to bring about a change for the better in our relationship.

It was an afternoon snack, actually. She was in the hospital for some tests on her heart, and I decided to visit one day and bring her favorite afternoon snack—a cruller and a coffee with lots of cream from her favorite donut shop. It was the right thing to do, but I wasn't looking forward to the visit. I anticipated a meal again surrounded by bitterness and strife. The Lord had to take me firmly by the hand and compel me forward into the hospital, bag of goodies at the ready.

When I reached her room, she was not there—and I was relieved. This was even better. I could leave the treat with a note wishing her well, and retreat with my conscience clear. I put down the bag on her bedside table, yet even as I reached for a pen in my bag, I sensed a word more than heard it. *Wait.*

Ugh. That could only be the Spirit's prompting. *Wait.* My least favorite thing to do anyway, and for this task, it just seemed to prolong what was to come. When I checked in at the nurse's station, there was a reference to the tests and a vague notion of how long that would take. Minutes? Hours? In the world of hospitals, there always seems to be very little certainty about the timeline. I paced her small room, looking alternately at my watch and out the window.

Finally, I heard her voice, and the nurse navigated her into the room via a wheelchair. My mother-in-law took one look at me, held out her hand, and burst into tears.

This, I had not expected. I had never seen her cry. The nurse wheeled her close to me and left us. I gripped her hand hard, my other hand giving her as much of a hug as one can when there's a wheelchair involved. "I'm so scared," she whispered. Then she told me tomorrow a pacemaker would be implanted. We both knew this was a good thing for her health, but surgery scared her, and no one had been with her when the doctor delivered the news.

After a good cry, I opened the bag and took out our coffee and crullers. "I'll be here tomorrow," I promised. "You won't be alone. Now, let's see if I picked the right donut for you." And we ate that meal together in peace.

That day, God prompted a visit with a treat to someone I thought could use a visit. It turns out it was I who needed to go. In that moment of vulnerability, I was able to see my mother-in-law as a fellow sufferer and forgive the past hurts I'd held on to for far too long.

Meals together are never just about the food, are they? In this case, it was a meal that was equal parts pardon, forgiveness, surrender, and vulnerability. It reminded me of the great act of reparation always available to us.

Worth Every Ingredient

RACHEL MCRAE

. . . .

Indeed, the very hairs of your head are all numbered. Don't be afraid; you are worth more than many sparrows.

Luke 12:7

The dream: planning a meal and creating the grocery list of items needed. Setting the table with matching dishes, nice silverware, and glasses. Using your favorite cookware and kitchen gadgets to prep and assemble each dish. Serving a nice hot meal to be enjoyed by your family that has gathered around the table as you swap stories about everyone's day.

The reality: pulling out the same handful of recipes every other week because they are easy to cut in half or to create just one serving of. Looking at the pretty bakeware in the cabinet that would be ideal for serving a crowd but reaching for the smallest casserole dish to cook up a single piece of chicken. Plating it alongside a hodgepodge of leftover vegetables and shuffling over to the recliner with a pillow as your tabletop and eating another meal by yourself in front of the evening news.

Being single at the age when most of my friends' kids are in college was never part of the dream I had for my life. Thankfully, the Lord has filled my life in countless ways that I never could have predicted, and I lead a very contented life (okay, I *mostly* lead a contented life). However, there are occasional days when my singleness seems to scream the loudest. And it's usually when I'm in the kitchen trying to figure out what to cook for this party of one.

Many times, when these cooking slumps hit, I wallow in the pity party and end up making something that's not the best for me or pouring a bowl of cereal. I have a cabinet full of cookbooks and recipe cards for wonderful meals. My Pinterest account mostly consists of food ideas. It's not that I'm at a loss as to what to make; that's certainly not the issue.

My problem is that I feel it's not worth it to go through all the planning, prepping, and time to cook a full meal for just one person. What if I don't like it? What a waste it would be. Or if I do like the dish, is it something I really want to eat leftovers of for the next three days?

Not too long ago, as I was starting to feel this familiar weight of woe descending upon my kitchen and in my heart, I heard the Holy Spirit whisper to me, *You think going through all the preparation and time is not worth it for one person, but the truth is, you think you're not worth the effort or the joy of a nice meal. But, oh, you are worth it and so much more.* I tried to brush the idea aside and reach for a cereal box, but I realized he was right.

I honestly love to cook. I enjoy making favorite recipes that remind me of my family and discovering new ones that I happily add to my repertoire of meals. I also like cooking and baking for friends and family who visit or taking food to a friend in need. But it wasn't until this kitchen confessional time with the Lord that I learned the bigger lesson of the importance of my own self-worth and how it extends way beyond the number of people I cook for. The life I lead is valuable, important, and beautiful. Yes, having a family of my own would be a wonderful blessing, too, but that doesn't mean my life as a single adult isn't just as meaningful and worth living to the fullest.

Finding the joy in cooking for one comes and goes, but I'm rediscovering it more often these days. I treat myself to the occasional steak. I get excited about a new recipe that calls for spices I don't already have in the pantry. I use my nicer dishes and glasses more often. Sure, I'm still sitting in my recliner with my pillow in my lap as my table, but it's an improvement in my dining experience and in my personal self-worth.

Whether you are a household of one or of many, find ways to add some fun and fancy to your routine meals. Play around with ingredients. Pick a country and find some recipes to try from their culture. Break out the nice dishes every now and then. If you want to get really crazy, use cloth napkins! Just find ways to treat yourself in these simple, everyday ways. Because you're worth it.

From Empty to Filled

ELIZABETH BERGET

· · · ·

He will tend his flock like a shepherd; he will gather the lambs in his arms; he will carry them in his bosom, and gently lead those that are with young.

Isaiah 40:11 ESV

I run laps around the dining room table, rescuing a tossed sippy cup for the baby and doling out more raspberries for the screeching toddler. In between my cutting grapes into tiny pieces and navigating the preschooler's big feelings about his sandwich having been cut into triangles instead of squares, the toddler manages to squeeze an applesauce pouch all over herself and somehow, even more improbably, the dog. Just as I finish wiping up the applesauce, the baby reaches full volume; it's time for a nap. I snag a few raspberries and one-fourth of the rejected sandwich on our way to his room.

Minutes later, he and I are sitting in the dark quiet. I nurse him in the rocker, my ears straining for any sign of trouble outside the door, where my older two are supposed to be playing quietly. I feel stretched like a spoke, pulled in too many directions to stay centered. I nurse him into sleepiness, and meanwhile, I realize I am *hungry*.

The morning began like most mornings, with the starter pistol of the baby's cry for milk, spilled cereal, and soggy diapers. I had curled my white knuckles around my coffee cup as though hanging on for dear life when my husband ducked out the door for work. I barely heard his *goodbye* over the din of blocks being stacked and knocked over on the living room floor. My breakfast had been a few handfuls of cereal straight from the box.

In the blackout-curtain dark of the nursery, I tally what I have managed to feed myself since the morning, and I come up woefully and calorically short. Since the early morning, I have ridden a tilt-a-whirl of my children's needs, changing jammies and diapers, wiping faces and hands, playing Candyland one-handed while nursing, and wiping the occasional tears from yet another toddler meltdown. I am not resentful. I am just tired . . . and admittedly grubby in yesterday's clothes and Monday's unwashed hair. I have been feeding people, in more ways than one, the entire day. Yet I remain hungry.

I have often wondered if God ever felt like a run-down mother in the Old Testament, serving up manna to a chorus of complaints, shaking his head and sighing as some of his children went out to gather on the Sabbath when he had specifically told them not to. But even from the very beginning of Genesis, we see a God who deeply cares for the bodies of his children, especially their hunger. Some of God's first recorded words to Adam are, "You are free to eat from any tree in the garden" (Gen. 2:16), as if God himself was intimately familiar with how toddlers somehow always wake up ravenous.

In John 21, we see Jesus caring for his followers' bodies on the beach, cooking up a simple breakfast for his bewildered and famished disciples, and I think every mother can deeply relate with God's care for Elijah in 1 Kings 19, when he offers the discouraged prophet a snack, a drink, and not one but two naps.

My eyes close along with the baby's. He has nursed his fill and is nearly asleep. In the rare moment of silence, I am suddenly filled with Jesus's words: "I am the bread of life. Whoever comes to me will never go hungry, and whoever believes in me will never be thirsty" (John 6:35).

In this season of caring for littles, I hunger for much—for hot coffee and uninterrupted sleep and, often, simply for a break—but I take comfort in knowing a God who not only understands my deep hunger but also promises to fill me with his own unending abundance when I turn to him in my need. In Jesus's words, I find myself fed as I feed my kids, cared for as I care for them, filled as I empty myself again and again for them. I know that, far more abundantly than the other three-fourths of dried-out sandwich waiting for me, God is ever present in my carnival-ride days, ever ready to feed me in more ways than one.

QUICK AND SIMPLE WARM SALAD FOR ONE

This recipe is highly adaptable to use what you have on hand. Almost any leftover or deli meat, hearty greens, nuts, dried fruit, or cheese could work.

Serves 1

1 Tbs olive oil
1–2 Tbs diced onion
⅔ cup 1-inch pieces green beans or asparagus
2 Tbs thinly sliced celery
2 slices deli ham, chopped (about ½ cup)
2 Tbs chopped unsalted pecans

2 Tbs dried cranberries
2 pieces curly kale, stems removed and chopped (about ¾ cup)
squeeze of fresh lemon juice
pinch of lemon zest
2 Tbs crumbled goat cheese
salt and pepper to taste

1. In a small pan (I like cast iron), heat olive oil over medium-high heat. Add onion and sauté for 2 minutes until softened and fragrant. Increase heat to high and add green beans. Cook for 4–5 minutes, allowing them to sit for 45 seconds or so between stirs so that they blister and char; sauté until just softened (watch so that the onions don't burn).

2. Decrease heat to medium. Add celery, ham, pecans, and dried cranberries and sauté for 1–2 minutes, allowing the ham to sear and heat through. Finally, add chopped kale and cook for 1–2 minutes, until greens have shrunk and wilted.

3. Remove pan from heat. Squeeze lemon juice over the salad mixture; sprinkle with lemon zest and goat cheese. Stir to mix, adding salt and pepper to taste.

Note: you can use already cooked onions or green beans/asparagus in this recipe. Just reduce the cooking time in step 1 to only reheat these before continuing.

For God's Glory

ESSIE FAYE TAYLOR

. . . .

So whether you eat or drink or whatever you do, do it all for the glory of God.
1 Corinthians 10:31

As I licked the last crumb of peach cobbler from my lips, I couldn't contain the sigh of satisfaction that escaped my mouth. I had captured every morsel eagerly, and now I was completely satisfied. Each bite was flavorful and delicious—made with love for my family. Smiles filled the crowded yet silent table. All of us were busy devouring the scrumptious dish. A part of the "clean plate club," we all then relaxed into a familiar time of sharing, game playing, and jest. There's no place like home; in many cases a good meal is "home."

It's comforting to know that our incredible God gets glory when we are satisfied, filled with happiness, and enjoying life. The thought that the God of the universe—our Creator—finds pleasure in our fellowship over a hearty meal brings me joy. Some people like to envision God our Savior as a distant God seated on heaven's throne concerned only with "spiritual things." It excites me, however, to know that my Savior is concerned about every aspect of my life—from the minute to the mega events. He *cares* about me—even down to the meals I devour. He cares about what feeds my soul.

Soul feeding can come in many shapes. Whatever satisfies your innermost being feeds your soul. This, of course, includes spiritual food: God's Word, prayer and communion with him, corporate study, prayer, fellowship, and other spiritual disciplines. In addition, our passions, dreams, desires, wishes, and pastimes feed our souls. So do our relationships and our self-care practices—including our diet. Our sovereign Lord cares about this, and we bring him glory as we take good care of our bodies, which "are God's temple" (1 Cor. 3:16), and nourish those around us.

In the text above, the apostle Paul addresses the believers at Corinth concerning a debate about whether or not to eat food sacrificed to idols. There was a question about what believers should eat or abstain from eating. In essence, the apostle advises believers to do everything to bring honor to God—this includes eating. I love eating so much that I am joyful to know that something that brings me such pleasure can also be used to bring joy and pleasure to my Lord. When we nourish ourselves, we are honoring God as we honor and care for our bodies as his stewards.

Call to action:

1. Practice being mindful of God's presence in every aspect of your life, from the minute to the mega.
2. Eat joyfully—enjoy your food. God is smiling as you enjoy and nourish your body and feed your soul. You should smile too.
3. Embrace what feeds your soul and bask in it; explore your interests, including but not limited to food choice. Be open-minded.
4. Search the Scriptures for what things please God. Learn them and get to know him more deeply.
5. Remember, when you acknowledge God, he will direct your path. Divine purpose, order, and appointments will come into your life.

Potatoes of Praise

LINDSEY SPOOLSTRA

• • • •

Then God said, "I've given you every sort of seed-bearing plant on Earth and every kind of fruit-bearing tree, given them to you for food. To all animals and all birds, everything that moves and breathes, I give whatever grows out of the ground for food." And there it was. God looked over everything he had made; it was so good, so very good! It was evening, it was morning—Day Six.

Genesis 1:29–31 Message

Last summer I grew my own potatoes for the first time. Blue ones. In two large buckets. I don't have a big yard, and much of what I do have is pleasantly shady, so my vegetable gardening is always an exercise in creativity. I won't say my diminutive plants did great, but they did yield me a pound or two of the freshest, crispiest, tastiest little spuds I've ever had.

Yes, I ate one raw, like an apple. It was that good. So good a Scripture came to mind—"Taste and see that the LORD is good" (Ps. 34:8)—which really isn't about literal food at all, but still. In that moment, what was on my tongue did indeed proclaim the Lord's goodness to me, and that moment of eating became also a moment of worship.

We're used to thinking about worship as what comes out of our mouths, in both word and song. But here's another Scripture to take (slightly) out of context: "So whether you eat or drink or whatever you do, do it all for the glory of God" (1 Cor. 10:31).

We can also worship in our everyday eating, and not just by thanking God for our daily bread. How? How do we praise the Lord not just *for* what he has given us but *by* what we put into our mouths?

I think one answer is by eating real food.

Modern processed foods are engineered to make us eat and crave and never be satisfied. Why do we consume such things? (Yes, they're tasty. I know. I'm not immune to the siren song of Oreos.) One reason, I think, is that we've been inundated with the message that eating real food is too difficult and takes too much time. We're too tired and too busy, and we deserve something convenient and easy.

Yet true ease isn't found in any engineering of humankind but only in the countercultural, upside-down way of Jesus. "Come to me, all you who are weary and burdened," he tells us, "and I will give you rest. Take my yoke upon you and learn from me, for I am gentle and humble in heart, and you will find rest for your souls. For my yoke is easy and my burden is light" (Matt. 11:28–30).

The world's way of convenience and hurry can never satisfy us. As Christians, we know this. But we often relegate this truth to the "big" things of life—salvation and eternity and all that Sunday stuff. We sometimes forget it also applies to the "small" things. What about literal thirst and hunger? What about that blue packet of Oreos versus that crunchy little blue potato?

In other words, how do we live out the Good News in our eating?

We could talk about the "don'ts," the negatives—factory farms and food deserts and preventable health issues and toxic diet culture—but let's not. Not now. This is a moment of worship, of praising the goodness of the Lord. Of eating the raw potato.

It doesn't have to be complicated. In fact, if it is complicated, maybe we're doing it wrong. As an aspect of living out the gospel—which, after all, is about being as a "little child" (Mark 10:14–15)—eating can be simple. And mindful. We partake of the Lord's good garden, and we praise his holy name.

> This is the [potato] the LORD has made;
> We will rejoice and be glad in it. (Ps. 118:24 NKJV)

CAULI POTATO CURRY

Adapted from the Kitchn.[*]

Serves 4

1 sm cauliflower (or about 1 lb florets)
1 tsp olive oil
1 lg onion, diced
1 tsp salt, divided
1 lb red, blue, or yellow potatoes, diced
3–5 cloves garlic (to taste), minced
1–2 tsp minced or grated fresh ginger

1 tsp cumin
2 tsp curry powder
1 (28 oz) can diced tomatoes in
 their juices (or 4 cups diced fresh
 tomatoes)
¼ cup plain yogurt (optional)

1. Chop cauliflower into small florets, and dice the tender parts of the stem as well (you should have about 4 cups). Heat olive oil in a large skillet or dutch oven over medium heat. Cook the onion with half of the salt until softened, then add potatoes and remaining salt. When potatoes are browning a bit, add cauliflower and cook until browned in spots.

2. Add garlic, ginger, cumin, and curry, and stir until fragrant, about 30 seconds or so. Pour in the tomatoes and their juices, scraping the bottom of the pan to loosen any browned bits if needed. Increase heat to medium-high and bring to a boil, then cover, reduce heat, and simmer for 15–20 minutes or until vegetables have softened.

3. For a thicker curry, leave uncovered the last 5 minutes or so of cooking. Turn off heat and stir in yogurt (if using). Taste and adjust seasoning, and serve with a cooked grain such as farro or rice, if desired. Bonus garnishes: chopped fresh cilantro, raisins, your favorite chutney, and/or roasted chickpeas.

* Emma Christensen, "Quick Recipe: Potato and Cauliflower Curry," the Kitchn, February 10, 2010, https://www.thekitchn.com/weeknight-recipe-potato-and-ca-108287.

Glorifying God in Our Bodies

KATHY-ANN C. HERNANDEZ

. . . .

Do you not know that your bodies are temples of the Holy Spirit, who is in you, whom you have received from God? You are not your own.

1 Corinthians 6:19

I am a big believer in "cooking from scratch," as we often say here in the United States.

As a Caribbean transplant, I come by it honestly; home cooking is a foundational element of our cosmopolitan culture. In the twin island Republic of Trinidad and Tobago where I grew up, we slow down every Sunday to prepare Sunday lunch. This is a meal that usually begins with an early morning trip to the market. With baskets in hand, men and women, often with children in tow, spend time haggling with their favorite vendors over produce and chatting with neighbors and even strangers all on the same mission. The meal preparation continues at home and often requires other family members pitch in to shell pigeon peas, clean dasheen leaves, grate coconut, clean soursop, and on and on. Later in the day, the family sits down in joyful camaraderie "ole talking" and enjoying the taste of their "sweet hands."

Like me, my American-born husband comes from a family with a long tradition of cooking from scratch. When we reminisce about days gone by, he often speaks with pride of his Great-Aunt Elsie, a master cook. Aunt Elsie's pound cake and mushroom veggie burgers are legendary. When Mark and I were dating, I had heard of and tasted, from the hands of her great-niece, a piece of Aunt Elsie's famous pound cake. Oh, my goodness! Deliciousness on a plate! However, I dared not ask for the recipe; it was only shared with family members—a part of Aunt Elsie's much-treasured legacy and part of the family's collective wealth. Finally, after Mark and I were married, this prized family heirloom was passed on to me.

And so, it is no surprise that my husband and I make time to cook from scratch at our house. It's not always convenient, and it definitely takes up much time, but it is "good time." It is time that allows us to slow down. As my husband and I putter around the kitchen, assisted by our two daughters, we find we are cooking up more than what's on the menu. We are continuing to add to the chain of generational wealth by passing on important cultural traditions. We are creating memories and opportunities to express ourselves creatively. We are also modeling for the girls what we value, teaching an important life skill, and reminding them not to outsource their own nutrition.

But more importantly, I have come to think of this ritual of cooking one's own food as an act of worship. We honor God when we model our nutrition according to his plan for our lives. Healthy and wholesome food was his originally recommended diet for us: "See, I have given you every herb that yields seed which is on the face of all the earth, and every tree whose fruit yields seed; to you it shall be for food" (Gen. 1:29 NKJV).

Many years later, in his first letter to the Corinthians, Paul advises followers of Christ, "So whether you eat or drink or whatever you do, do it all for the glory of God" (1 Cor. 10:31). He also says to them, "Don't you realize that your body is the temple of the Holy Spirit, who lives in you and was given to you by God? You do not belong to yourself" (6:19 NLT). This imagery is striking—our bodies are temples in which God's Holy Spirit longs to dwell.

I cannot think of a more intimate act of taking care of the temples God has given us than choosing to be intentional about what we put into them—how we feed them. The food we eat has the capacity either to sharpen our minds or to dull our senses in a way that inhibits our ability to connect with the divine presence in our lives.

When we make time to cook our own food, we are able to develop an intimate appreciation for the food that we eat and the Creator of all living things. In sum, we honor God when we take time to feed our bodies well. This act of worship is something I value greatly, and it is a practice that I hope to pass on to the next generation of Aunt Elsie's.

Eat and Be Merry

ESSIE FAYE TAYLOR

. . . .

Go, eat your food with gladness, and drink your wine with a joyful heart, for God has already approved what you do.

Ecclesiastes 9:7

My heart was full of dreams and doubt. I was certain about the gifts God had entrusted to me. Yet I was incredibly afraid to bet on myself and step out of the boat of comfort and walk the uncertain waters of life in order to cultivate my God-given gifts and abilities. I was paralyzed by fear, and my mind was overcome with what-ifs. What if I failed? What if I stepped out of the comfy boat onto turbulent waters and began to sink? What if others laughed at my dreams or didn't approve of them? All of these questions kept me from pursuing my passions and sharing them with the world for God's glory.

What I failed to see was that, just like in the apostle Peter's case, Jesus was—and is—present with me. He will guide and sustain me. He will feed my soul because he already approves of what I do. With God's blessing, life's possibilities and opportunities are endless. "I can do all things through Christ who strengthens me" (Phil. 4:13 NKJV).

In the text, King Solomon admonishes us to enjoy our food with gladness. He advises that we get joy and rest in the fact God has provided for us—and, more importantly, has already approved of our actions. Your thoughts birth actions, and actions in turn birth habits. Ultimately, habits birth character. God approves of our Christlike character. When God approves of us, he sanctions a blessing upon us. The blessing commanded by God brings prosperity, hope, joy, peace, protection, and provision—it makes us happy. So Solomon tells us to rest in God's provision and to be joyful that we have God's blessing upon us.

There are few things that bring joy like a good meal. While eating, I have been known to break into a joyful song or dance. Not only do flavorful dishes make the taste buds dance, but that joy translates throughout the entire body. It is the same with feeding the soul—you might likely break into a joyful dance. Just ask King David, who danced for joy before the Lord. He danced so vigorously with joy and gladness that his wife at the time was embarrassed. However, there is nothing embarrassing about dancing before the Lord. Praise and worship feed the soul and give thanks to God for his goodness.

King Solomon, as an older man of experience and wisdom, teaches several notable lessons gained from his years of walking with God from his youth through various stages of life. First, he emphasizes the importance of gladness, joy, and contentment. As a young king, Solomon was content with the presence of God. When in the presence of God, instead of asking for great riches, he asked for knowledge and wisdom of how to faithfully serve God and his people. As a result, God granted his request and gave him riches and wisdom untold. Second, Solomon encourages believers to find contentment in approval from God. He is clear: maybe people don't approve of what you do, but God has already approved of what you do. So be glad.

Call to action:

1. Be grateful for the provision of God in your life.
2. Enjoy God's provision and be glad. Be joyful and happy for what God supplies, and thank him.
3. Find contentment in Christ. Practice gratitude daily. Keeping a gratitude journal is a way to record your blessings and be thankful.
4. Rest in God's approval of you. Pleasing God is most important in this life and the life to come. As believers, our ultimate goal is to hear our Father say, "Well done, my good and faithful servant." The blessed news is that we don't have to wait until eternity to hear him say it.
5. Remember, we have much to be happy about. God is cheering you on; he's in your corner. He is eagerly waiting to bless you and shower you with love.

A Royal Invitation

RACHEL MCRAE

. . . .

"Hallelujah! For our Lord God Almighty reigns. Let us rejoice and be glad and give him glory! For the wedding of the Lamb has come, and his bride has made herself ready. Fine linen, bright and clean, was given her to wear." . . . Then the angel said to me, "Write this: Blessed are those who are invited to the wedding supper of the Lamb!"

Revelation 19:6–9

Have you ever been invited to a formal meal by a host who has a really large home? As you walk in, you might start wondering if you are dressed appropriately or if you know how to make small talk with the host and their fancy guests. Will you fit in with everyone? And then the big worry of the evening: Will you know which silverware to use? Is there anything more intimidating than sitting down at a place setting that has utensils you have no idea what to do with?

The fanciest house I've had a meal in is Kensington Palace in London. Okay, it was afternoon tea, and it was in the public tearoom next to the gift shop at the palace, but I still think it counts. It was my last afternoon in England, and I was reflecting on my adventures with a hot cuppa and a fresh fruit scone. I found myself imagining what it would be like to be invited to a royal dinner at the palace. I'm sure the invitation would be printed on heavy stationery and would be hand delivered by the Royal Mail. I can picture myself staring at it in disbelief that my name was on the card. *They want me?* That would set off a chain of activities that would ensure I was palace ready. Goodness knows that even on my best day, I would not be pulled together enough to attend such a soiree. It would require a team of hairdressers, makeup artists, and wardrobe stylists to get me polished up to be worthy to stand in front of royalty.

It's fun to imagine ourselves being invited to the biggest parties, fanciest dinners, and most exclusive social gatherings. In reality, only a small handful lead the kind of life where they receive those invitations.

There's good news for them and for the rest of us. The best invitation to the most extravagant meal is extended to all of us. Through the life, death, and resurrection of Jesus Christ, God is inviting us to join him and all the church at the wedding banquet of the Lamb that is described in Revelation 19. I love the glimpse of eternity we receive here. When Jesus comes again, God wants us to party! It will be a feast unlike anything we can imagine.

It's also a banquet Jesus can't wait to attend himself (Matt. 26:29). Jesus, who sees and knows everything, is eager to join us at this party? Goodness, can you imagine just how awesome this event will be that even the Son of God is eager for the day?

When there are times on this side of heaven we feel forgotten and not invited to gatherings both small and large, just remember the banquet that is to come. It won't compare to any event that's happened before. It will blow this year's "party of the year" right out of the water. And you're invited.

In fact, the Host, who happens to be the King of the universe, wants all of us around that table. It wouldn't be the same without you. He's extending the invitation to you today to live your earthly life with him while we await our eternity with him. That will be one banquet you don't want to miss.

And don't worry. You won't have to worry over which fork to use when you get there.

ORANGE CRANBERRY SCONES

Yields 9–10 scones

2 cups all-purpose flour
1 Tbs baking powder
3 Tbs sugar
zest of 1 orange

½ tsp salt
5 Tbs unsalted butter, cold and cubed
½ cup dried cranberries, diced
1 cup heavy/whipping cream, cold

1. Preheat oven to 425°.

2. In a large bowl, whisk together flour, baking powder, sugar, orange zest, and salt.

3. Add the cold butter into the flour mixture by rubbing or smearing butter cubes between your fingertips as you toss them around in the flour mixture. Work fast, rubbing through all the big lumps of butter until the mixture resembles coarse bread crumbs. (You can also use two butter knives or a pastry blender for this step instead.)

4. Mix in diced dried cranberries.

5. Stir in cold cream with a spatula or fork until the dough comes together.

6. Transfer dough to a clean work surface and give it a few gentle kneads (less than 10) to make the dough come together.

7. Lightly flour your work surface and press dough into a 1–1½ inch (2–3 cm) thick round disk.

8. Lightly flour the surface of the dough and a 1½–2 inch (4 cm) round cutter and cut into pieces. Place the rounds, spacing them about an inch (3 cm) apart, onto a baking sheet lined with parchment paper. Press remaining scraps together and cut more pieces until the dough is used up. (You can also use a knife to cut the disk of scone dough into 10 equal wedges if you don't have a biscuit cutter.)

9. Bake scones on the middle rack of the oven for 12–15 minutes or until the tops are lightly golden brown. Place on a wire rack to cool.

Note: To get the scones to rise high and mighty, flour the cutter well and press it into the dough with a swift downward motion. Do not twist the cutter as you push it into the dough, as this will hamper the rise of the scones.

Recipe Index

Sides and Salads

Beet Barley Risotto   177
Choose Your Own Adventure Hummus   146
Colorful Greek Salad   168
Grandma Roggie's Apple Salad   136
Grilled Peach Salad   104
Kale and Farro Salad   160
Mama Love Mixed Veggie Casserole   140
Quick and Simple Warm Salad for One   250
Sisters' Signature Caesar   46
Spanish Rice   131
Sweet Fried Plantain   114
Tableside Guacamole   185

Soups and Stews

Black-Eyed Pea and Collard Stew   66
Country Vegetable Soup   223
Hobo Stew   123
Instant Pot Irish Beef Stew   202
Kale Soup   88
Martha's Hearty Beef Stew   93
Mom's Lentil Soup   207
Sancocho (Meat Stew with Root
    Vegetables)   30
Savory Comfort Chili to Share with
    Friends   215
Wild Rice Chicken Soup   151

Snacks

Choose Your Own Adventure Hummus   146
Jammy Granola Bars   235
Sweet Fried Plantain   114
Tableside Guacamole   185

Contributors

Alyssa Roggie Allen is a freelance writer and editor with more than twenty-five years of experience. She lives with her husband, Chad, and two teenagers in Grand Rapids, Michigan.

Chad R. Allen is a writer, speaker, editor, and writing coach. A twenty-year publishing professional, he has worked with many bestselling authors and leads BookCamp, a community and training center for writers. His passion is helping writers get their books into the world, and he blogs at ChadRAllen.com.

Helen Arnold, author and content creator, loves a good cup of tea while reading her *Not So Secret Love Letters*. Follow her on Instagram or TikTok @ NotSoSecretLoveLetters.

Amy Ballor is a copywriter and nature lover who loves doing life with her devoted husband, three charming kids, and many furry companions. She calls West Michigan home.

Erin Bartels is the award-winning author of *We Hope for Better Things*, *The Words between Us*, *All That We Carried*, *The Girl Who Could Breathe Under Water*, *Everything Is Just Beginning*, and *The Lady with the Dark Hair*. She has worked at Baker Publishing Group for more than twenty years, most of that time as a copywriter. Find her at ErinBartels.com.

Elizabeth Berget is a Minneapolis mama to three who primarily writes about faith and motherhood. You can read more of her work at ElizabethBerget.substack.com or on Instagram @Elizabeth_A_Berget.

Leslie M. Bosserman is a mom of three and has a calling to help others get unstuck as they turn ideas into action. She lives in Sacramento, California, and travels internationally for coaching, organizational trainings, and retreat facilitation. Learn more about her writing and speaking at LeslieMBosserman.com and follow her @LeadWithIntention.

Briggitte P. Brown is a busy mom of seven and grandmother to three. She has been married to her husband for twenty-four years. She is a Licensed Clinical Social Worker and owner of her group practice in New Britain, Connecticut. When she has quiet time, she enjoys blogging and writing. Learn more at AuthenticallyHealingPodcast.com.

Robin Bupp is avidly curious and loves to share what she learns with anyone who will listen; most often it's her husband, her kids, her small group, or her cats.

Connie Clyburn, coauthor of *Aging Fabulously: 52 Devotions Sure to Give You a Faith-Lift* and author of the children's book *Willy the Silly-Haired Snowman's Great Adventure*, is a blogger, award-winning journalist, and avid researcher who hails from the Tennessee backroads. Learn more at DoublewideWisdom.com.

Marla Darius is a wife, mom of five, photographer, nurse, speaker, and author. She lives in Connecticut and loves to read outside in the sunshine.

Brianna DeWitt reads, enjoys tacos with her friends, and bakes her nieces' and nephews' birthday cakes in Grand Rapids, Michigan. She believes desserts are best with chocolate and peanut butter.

Andrea Doering is a publishing professional who enjoys reading, writing, and definitely cooking.

Jennifer Drummond, a spiritual director and poet, writes about the seasons from her home in Hamilton, Massachusetts. Find her writing at JADrummond.com.

Jenni Elwood hosts *The Refuge* podcast and is the author of *Counting Up to Christmas* and *24 Gifts from the Gospel of Luke*. She's a travel fanatic and coffee addict and enjoys nerding out on biblical context. Learn more at JenniferElwood.com.

Jenny Erlingsson, author of *Her Part to Play*, writes romantic fiction and creative nonfiction in the margins of marriage, motherhood, and ministry in Iceland. Learn more at JennyErlingsson.com.

Kristen D. Farrell is a teacher, speaker, and aspiring writer and spends as much time in nature as possible, preferably around a campfire with her family in the Adirondack Mountains. She resides in Buffalo, New York. Follow her on Instagram @KristenInTheWorld.

Tammy Gerhard is a wife, mom, friend, author, speaker, mentor, and trained counselor. She resides in Manchester, Connecticut, where she co-owns a coffee shop in the center of town.

Nicola Gordon loves to study God's Word and write and speak to his glory. She makes her home in Ontario, Canada, where she is a devoted wife and mother of two adult sons.

Emma Greydanus is a publishing professional who enjoys fresh-baked cookies, a strong cup of coffee, and honoring God through the written word. She resides in Michigan.

Kathy-Ann C. Hernandez, PhD, is the author of *Waiting by the Brook: Seven Steps to Deeper Intimacy with God* and the founder of Value What Matters. Learn more at ValueWhatMatters.com.

Lisa Larsen Hill is passionate about sharing messages of hope, faith, and love. She is an author, biblical storyteller, and speaker. Learn more at LisaLarsenHill.com.

April Johnson, the author of *I Am Hope* and *I Am Enough: God Made Me Enough*, enjoys writing children's books promoting self-esteem and faith. Learn more at AJCreativeWrites.com.

Tyra Lane-Kingsland is a speaker, author, and mama of six who delights in encouraging women. Learn more at InspiredToLiveFully.com.

Bethany Lenderink is an editor, aspiring writer, and dog mom. You can check out more of her writing on Facebook at OnPaperI'mAnAdult or on her website, BethanyLenderink.com.

Kimberly Leonard and her husband enjoy life with family and friends along the Colorado Front Range. She is currently working toward her licensure as an MFT.

Maria Leonard is the mother to six unique and fabulous kids, a seasoned military spouse, and wife of twenty-nine years to her man, Brook. She lives in Colorado, where she spends most of her time behind the wheel of a big van providing sideline and academic support for some of her favorite people.

Lekeisha Maldon is a devotional author, wife, momma, and lover of Jesus. She currently resides in North Carolina. Follow her on Instagram @LekeishaMaldon or visit WalkTheNarrowWay.com.

Jessica Mathisen, author of *An Overwhelming Hope*, lives just outside of Atlanta, Georgia, with her husband and three kids. You can follow her on Instagram @JessicaNMathisen or visit JessicaNMathisen.com.

Rachel McRae is a publishing professional with twenty-five years of getting good books into the hands of readers. You'll usually find her reading, hiking, or watching college football at her home in Nashville, Tennessee.

Catherine (Cathee) Miles is a retired clergyperson who enjoys mentoring, teaching Bible studies, and leading prayer ministry. She loves her family, church, and playing pickleball. She has written devotionals for Advent and Lent and is working on a yearlong devotional describing the journey to holy living.

Maureen Miller loves to encourage others through the written word and is an award-winning author. She writes for *Guideposts* and her local newspaper, and she blogs about God's extraordinary character discovered in ordinary things.

With her husband, Bill, she's raised three wonderful children and is now enjoying grands on their hobby homestead in western North Carolina. Learn more at PenningPansies.com.

Amy Nemecek is the author of *The Language of the Birds and Other Poems*. She loves gathering around the table with family and friends—especially when someone else does the cooking!

Jill Noble writes to strengthen the weary, embolden the fearful, and encourage the faithful. She delights in pointing others to Jesus, the Author and Sustainer of our life stories. Learn more at JillNoble.me.

Meghann and Rayce Patterson are a recently married couple settling into Grand Rapids, Michigan, who love to use food as a way to build community with others.

Olivia Peitsch is a booklover turned publishing professional with more than ten years in the industry. A bookworm by day and a baking enthusiast by night, Olivia is also lucky enough to add the titles of wife and mother into the mix.

Karynthia Glasper Phillips is an author and speaker with a passion for women to practice self-care for a healthy spirit, mind, and body to effectively answer the call of purpose in their lives. Follow her on Facebook at Karynthia Glasper Phillips or on Instagram @Karynthia_QuietTime.

Donna Pryor, author *of Bone of My Bones and Flesh of My Flesh*, enjoys writing family-focused devotionals. Learn more at DailyDivineDates.com.

Katie M. Reid is a speaker and author of *Made Like Martha* and *A Very Bavarian Christmas*. She is also the cohost of *The Martha + Mary Show* podcast. Katie enjoys cut-to-the-chase conversations with friends and getting creative with recipes. Connect with Katie on Instagram @Katie_M_Reid or at KatieMReid.com.

Maggie Wallem Rowe is a national speaker and dramatist who writes from Peace Ridge, her home in the Great Smoky Mountains of western North Carolina. The author of *This Life We Share* and *Life Is Sweet, Y'all*, Maggie loves keeping her family fed. Visit her at MaggieRowe.com.

Darcy Schock writes stories for people who want more hope in a brighter tomorrow, freedom to unlock the person God created them to be, and confidence to live it out. You can find out more at DarcySchock.com.

Marianne Shehata is an author, educator, and speaker. She is an avid foodie who enjoys entertaining, traveling, and mentoring the younger generations. She delights in the multicultural flavors of her vibrant city, Toronto, Ontario.

Lindsey Spoolstra is a lifetime Michigander and twenty-year publishing veteran who can generally be found outdoors, in her kitchen, or in other places of worship.

Cindy K. Sproles is an author, speaker, and conference teacher. She is the cofounder of Christian Devotions Ministries, a life coach, and a writing mentor with Writing Right Author Mentoring Service. Cindy is the director of the Asheville Christian Writers Conference, held yearly at the Billy Graham Training Center in Asheville, North Carolina. Learn more at CindySproles.com.

Rhonda Stoppe is host of the *Old Ladies Know Stuff* podcast and is a bestselling author of seven books, including *Moms Raising Sons to Be Men*. Learn more at RhondaStoppe.com.

Kristen Strong, author of *Girl Meets Change, Back Roads to Belonging*, and *When Change Finds You*, writes as a friend offering meaningful encouragement for each season of life so you can see it with more hope and less worry. She and her US Air Force veteran husband, David, have three children. You can find her at KristenStrong.com, DaySpring's (in)courage, and on Instagram @KristenStrong.

Shelly Sulfridge is a Southern gal living in Alaska, an aspiring writer, and a missionary. Shelly comes from a long line of storytellers and loves writing with humor. Find her on Instagram @ShellySulfridge and on Facebook at Shelly Sulfridge, and sign up for her author newsletter at ShellySulfridge.com.

Essie Faye Taylor is the author of *Finding the Love You Deserve: 30 Lessons in Self-Love & Acceptance*. As a language educator, she enjoys teaching, wordplay, and writing from her home in Chicago. Follow her on Instagram @The_Essie_Faye.

Kit Tosello, author of *The Color of Home*, enjoys writing bighearted small-town stories featuring hope and humor. Visit KitTosello.com.

Emily Uebbing lives in West Michigan with her husband and their energetic shepsky. She will go out of her way for ice cream.

Katelyn Van Kooten is a children's author and freelance writer who works in the publishing industry. A diehard Michigander, she can usually be found in her Grand Rapids home, reading a novel and drinking too much coffee. Find her on Instagram @KVKWriter.

Jill V. Woodward is a writer and gardener who loves gathering assorted people to share meals together at her home in northwest Georgia.

Kaila Yim is a writer and loves to host others in her home in Minnesota. She enjoys blogging on KailaYim.com.

Courtney Zonnefeld is a Michigan-based editor and writer who loves exploring the world through stories, songs, and recipes. Follow her on Instagram @ ZonnefeldWords.

Naomi Zylstra enjoys reading, writing, and baking in her free time. She and her husband call West Michigan home.